To "see ourselves as others see us . . . "

Professor of Law at Columbia University, Telford Taylor was America's chief counsel for the prosecution at the Nazi war-crimes trials at Nuremberg in 1946. He holds the rank of brigadier general, and served in various official capacities during the Roosevelt and Truman administrations.

In NUREMBERG AND VIETNAM: AN AMERICAN TRAGEDY, General Taylor ranges across the entire history of the laws of war, their relevance at Nuremberg and their application to Vietnam. Profound and thoughtful, he explores the troubling questions raised by America's course in Southeast Asia.

Telford Taylor penetrates the conscience of his country.

# Nuremberg and Vietnam: An American Tragedy

## by Telford Taylor

BANTAM BOOKS
TORONTO · NEW YORK · LONDON
A NATIONAL GENERAL COMPANY

*This low-priced Bantam Book
has been completely reset in a type face
designed for easy reading, and was printed
from new plates. It contains the complete
text of the original hard-cover edition.*
NOT ONE WORD HAS BEEN OMITTED.

NUREMBERG AND VIETNAM:
AN AMERICAN TRAGEDY

*A Bantam Book / published by arrangement with
The New York Times Company*

PRINTING HISTORY
*Quadrangle edition published 1970
Bantam edition published May 1971*

ACKNOWLEDGMENTS
*The excerpt on pages 197-198 is from* The Military Half, *copyright
© 1969 by Jonathan Schell by permission of Alfred A. Knopf, Inc.*

*The excerpt on page 125 is from* One Morning In The War, *copyright © 1970 by Richard Hammer by permission of Coward-McCann, Inc.*

*Several quotes in Chapter 5 attributed to Richard A. Falk are from*
The Vietnam War And International Law, *Volume I, copyright ©
1968. Edited by Richard A. Falk by permission of Princeton University Press.*

*Published simultaneously in the United States and Canada*

*To the Flag*
*and*
*The Liberty and Justice*
*For Which It Stands*

# Contents

*The soldier, be he friend or foe, is charged
with the protection of the weak and unarmed.
It is the very essence and reason for his being.
When he violates this sacred trust, he not
only profanes his entire cult but threatens the
very fabric of international society. The
traditions of fighting men are long and
honorable. They are based upon the noblest
of human traits—sacrifice.*

—GEN. DOUGLAS MACARTHUR, 1946, confirming the
death sentence imposed by a United States military
commission on General Tomayuki Yamashita.

## Introduction

A QUARTER OF A CENTURY has passed since
Robert H. Jackson, speaking for the United States
of America, opened the war crimes trials of Nazi
German leaders at Nuremberg.

The event cast a long shadow into the future. In
Germany, war crimes trials arising from the Second
World War are being held to this very day. In the
United States, far from being forgotten, the Nuremberg trials are invoked today, not in connection
with a war that is ancient history to everyone under
50, but as part of the seething, anguished debate
over the war in Vietnam, which is shaking our
society to its foundations.

"While this law is first applied against German
aggressors," said Jackson in his address to the
Nuremberg tribunal, "if it is to serve any useful

purpose it must condemn aggression by any other nations, including those which sit here now in judgment." As he spoke those words, many eyes in the courtroom shifted to the faces of the two Soviet members of the court, the judicial representatives of a country that had invaded Poland in 1939 and Finland in 1940 and was widely believed to have been responsible in 1941 for the slaughter of thousands of Polish prisoners-of-war in the Katyn forest. That Jackson's admonition went unheeded by the Russians in later years—Hungary in 1956, Czechoslovakia in 1968—has been the general opinion in the United States. After years of the Iron Curtain and the Berlin wall, most Americans have no more difficulty in condemning aggressions and atrocities by the Reds today than they did in the past when brown and black uniformed Nazis and Fascists were the culprits.

But now the wheel has spun full circle, and the fingers of accusation are pointed not at others for whom we have felt scorn and contempt, but at ourselves. Worse yet, many of the pointing fingers are our own. Voices of the rich and poor and black and white, strident voices and scholarly voices, all speaking our own tongue, raise question of the legality under the Nuremberg principles of our military actions in Vietnam, and in Cambodia as well. Accounts of the conduct of American troops, especially at Son My in March, 1968, have stung the national conscience as nothing else since the days of slavery, and again Nuremberg is invoked as the symbol of condemnation.

What are the Nuremberg legal principles, and

what is their meaning today as applied to American involvement in Vietnam? When we sent hundreds of thousands of troops to South Vietnam, bombed North Vietnam, and moved into Cambodia, were our national leaders as guilty of launching a war of aggression as were Hitler and his generals when they invaded Poland, or Belgium, or Greece, or other countries that were way-stations on the Nazi march of conquest? Will Son My go down in the history of man's inhumanity bracketed with Katyn, Lidice, Oradour, Malmédy, and other names that still ring sadly in the ears of those old enough to have heard the sound? More generally, are the people of the United States able to face the proposition that Jackson put forth in their name, and examine their own conduct under the same principles that they applied to the Germans and Japanese at the Nuremberg and other war crimes trials?

These are the questions this book will examine. In undertaking this discussion, I have endeavored to avoid assumptions and preconceptions as to how these questions should be answered, since I believe that they need to be considered quite as carefully and urgently by those who execute or support our Vietnam policies as by those in opposition.

For these purposes, the term "Nuremberg trials" should not be taken as limited to the precise rulings of the Nuremberg courts, but in its broad sense, as standing for all the war crimes trials that followed in the wake of the Second World War, and the ideas they have generated. Today, "Nuremberg" is both what actually happened there and what people think happened, and the second is more important than the first. To set the record straight is, no doubt, a useful historical exercise, but sea change is itself a reality, and it is not the bare record but the ethos of Nuremberg with which we must reckon today.

Put another way, Nuremberg is not only what was said and done there, but also what was said about it, then and subsequently. By no means all that has been said is favorable. The late Senator Robert A. Taft is the best remembered of Nuremberg's contemporaneous critics, largely because his statements won him an accolade in the late President Kennedy's widely read book, "Profiles in Courage." But the very fact that Taft was cited for bravery signifies the overwhelming praise and approbation that the American public bestowed on the trials at the time.[1] International approval was equally impressive; 23 nations adhered to the treaty under which the first Nuremberg trial was held, and after its conclusion the General Assembly of the United Nations affirmed "the principles of international law" embodied in the Nuremberg judgment.

As the principal sponsor, organizer and executant of the Nuremberg trials, the United States is more deeply committed to their principles than any other nation. Some of those in high places who brought about our military involvement in Vietnam are well aware of this, and have sought to justify their course of action on the basis of those very principles. When he was Secretary of State, Dean Rusk described the organization of a durable peace as "the great central question of our day," and de-

1. This and other footnotes begin on page 209.

clared that checking Communist aggression in Southeast Asia was essential to that aim. Walt Rostow, former special assistant to President Johnson, told a group of college student editors that our "intervention had been based legally on obligations under SEATO [Southeast Asia Treaty Organization] to resist aggression." As the editors of *Life* magazine put it in 1967: "Most Americans consider South Vietnam to be the victim of aggression and North Vietnam the aggressor. That is what the war is about." These justifications are all based on the view, with which the name of Nuremberg is now associated, that waging aggressive war is a crime.

Needless to say, many Americans do not entertain the views *Life* attributed to them, and fewer today than when the editorial was printed. The claim that American intervention in Vietnam is itself an aggressive war and therefore criminal—the so-called "Nuremberg defense"—has been put forward by draft card burners, draftees facing induction and soldiers about to be shipped to Vietnam. A young Army doctor, Captain Howard Levy, sought to justify his refusal to give medical training to Green Berets on the ground that his pupils would turn their training to criminal purposes. Since publication of eye-witness accounts of the American action at Son My, such contentions and defenses have multiplied. The North Vietnamese, too, have heard of Nuremberg, and recited its precedent as the basis for trying captured American aircraft pilots as war criminals—a project which Hanoi apparently has now abandoned.

If these several invocations of Nuremberg are

diverse and contradictory, that is no reason to dismiss the trials as meaningless. We do not scrap the Constitution because learned judges cannot agree on the interpretation of its provisions. All profound moral doctrine is broad enough so that its particular application generates controversy, as is manifest in the old saying about the Devil's ability to quote Scripture to his own purpose.

Furthermore, beneath these wildly divergent views of the Nuremberg precedent there is a common denominator: that there are some universal standards of human behavior that transcend the duty of obedience to national laws. "Your country, the United States, has established that a citizen must *not* go along with policies he believes to be wrong," we are admonished in a current leaflet[2]: *"That's what the Nuremberg Trials were all about!"*

As a legal and historical matter that is grossly overstated, but it is fairly representative of views about Nuremberg that are frequently expressed, especially by young people. Furthermore, although the statement is an exaggeration, it is not a total fabrication; the notion of individual accountability before the bar of international law lies at the heart of the Nuremberg judgments, and the reluctance of the Germans to resist oppressive acts of state is widely held to have greatly aided the Nazi seizure of power.

I have used the name "Nuremberg" in the title of this work because that is the label that time and usage have affixed to the set of principles and problems with which the book deals. But the usage is indicative of a prevalent but wholly mistaken notion that the Nuremberg trials were the original source of these principles. It is important to correct this misconception, for it distorts the entire matter by concealing the antiquity of these vexing questions, and the depth to which they permeate the moral and political history of mankind. Symbol though it be, Nuremberg is but one of many points of reference in the course of men's efforts to use law as a vehicle for mitigating the ravages of war, and eventually abolishing war itself.

Thus the true sources of today's crisis of conscience over our intervention in Vietnam, and the consequences it has entailed, long antedate the Second World War and the Nuremberg aftermath. Accordingly, I have devoted the first part of this book to a brief description and analysis of the major legal concepts upon which the Nuremberg and other war crimes trials are based. Thereafter I have endeavored to show what the Nuremberg experience contributed to the development of these concepts, and finally to examine their application to the Vietnam war, and to conscience-stabbing episodes such as those at Son My.

The reader will soon see that the questions are difficult, and that many are answered inadequately or not at all. But it is my hope that he will put down the book persuaded that, however they may be answered, these questions must be faced.

# 1 / War Crimes

WHAT IS A "WAR CRIME"? To say that it is a violation of the laws of war is true, but not very meaningful.

War consists largely of acts that would be criminal if performed in time of peace—killing, wounding, kidnapping, destroying or carrying off other peoples' property. Such conduct is not regarded as criminal if it takes place in the course of war, because the state of war lays a blanket of immunity over the warriors.*

But the area of immunity is not unlimited, and its boundaries are marked by the laws of war. Unless the conduct in question falls within those boun-

---

* This concept is very ancient; it is clearly stated by the 12th century compiler of canon law, Gratian: "The soldier who kills a man in obedience to authority is not guilty of murder."

daries, it does not lose the criminal character it would have should it occur in peaceful circumstances. In a literal sense, therefore, the expression "war crime" is a misnomer, for it means an act that remains criminal even though committed in the course of war, because it lies outside the area of immunity prescribed by the laws of war.

What, then, are the "laws of war"? They are of ancient origin, and followed two main streams of development. The first flowed from medieval notions of knightly chivalry. Over the course of the centuries the stream has thinned to a trickle; it had a brief spurt during the days of single-handed aerial combat, and survives today in rules (often violated) prohibiting various deceptions such as the use of the enemy's uniforms or battle insignia, or the launching of a war without fair warning by formal declaration.

The second and far more important concept is that the ravages of war should be mitigated as far as possible by prohibiting needless cruelties, and other acts that spread death and destruction and are not reasonably related to the conduct of hostilities. The seeds of such a principle must be nearly as old as human society, and ancient literature abounds with condemnation of pillage and massacre. In more recent times, both religious humanitarianism and the opposition of merchants to unnecessary disruptions of commerce have furnished the motivation for restricting customs and understandings. In the 17th century these ideas began to find expression in learned writings, especially those of the Dutch jurist-philosopher Hugo Grotius.

The formalization of military organization in the 18th-century brought the establishment of military courts, empowered to try violations of the laws of war as well as other offenses by soldiers. During the American Revolution, both Captain Nathan Hale and the British Major John André were convicted as spies and ordered to be hanged, the former by a British military court and the latter by a "Board of General Officers" appointed by George Washington. During the Mexican War, General Winfield Scott created "military commissions," with jurisdiction over violations of the laws of war committed either by American troops against Mexican civilians, or vice versa.[1]

Up to that time the laws of war had remained largely a matter of unwritten tradition, and it was the United States, during the Civil War, that took the lead in reducing them to systematic, written form. In 1863 President Lincoln approved the promulgation by the War Department of "Instructions for the Government of Armies of the United States in the Field," prepared by Francis Lieber, a German veteran of the Napoleonic wars, who emigrated to the United States and became professor of law and political science at Columbia University. These comprised 159 articles, covering such subjects as "military necessity," "punishment of crimes against the inhabitants of hostile countries," "prisoners of war," and "spies." It was by a military commission appointed in accordance with these instructions that Mary Surratt and the others accused of conspiring to assassinate Lincoln were tried.

In the wake of the Crimean War, the Civil War

and the Franco-Prussian War of 1870 there arose, in Europe and America, a tide of sentiment for codification of the laws of war and their embodiment in international agreements. The principal fruits of that movement were the series of treaties known today as the Hague and Geneva Conventions. For present purposes, the most important of these are the Fourth Hague Convention of 1907, and the Geneva Prisoner of War, Red Cross, and Protection of Civilians Conventions of 1929 and 1949.

"The right of belligerents to adopt means of injuring the enemy is not unlimited," declared Article 22 of the Fourth Hague Convention, and ensuing articles specify a number of limitations: Enemy soldiers who surrender must not be killed, and are to be taken prisoner; captured cities and towns must not be pillaged, nor "undefended" places bombarded; poisoned weapons and other arms "calculated to cause unnecessary suffering" are forbidden. Other provisions make it clear that war is not a free-for-all between the populations of the countries at war; only members of the armed forces can claim protection of the laws of war, and if a noncombatant civilian takes hostile action against the enemy he is guilty of a war crime. When an army occupies enemy territory, it must endeavor to restore public order, and respect "family honor and rights, the lives of persons, and private property, as well as religious convictions and practices."

Rules requiring humane treatment of prisoners, and for protection of the sick and wounded, are prescribed in the Geneva Conventions. While there is no general treaty on naval warfare, the Ninth

Hague Convention prohibited the bombardment of undefended "ports," and the London Naval Treaty of 1930 condemned submarine sinkings of merchant vessels, unless passengers and crews were first placed in "safety."

In all of these treaties, the laws of war are stated as general principles of conduct, and neither the means of enforcement nor the penalties for violations are specified. The substance of their provisions, however, has been taken into the military law of many countries, and is often set forth in general orders, manuals of instruction, or other official documents. In the United States, for example, the Lieber rules of 1863 were replaced in 1914 by an army field manual which, up-dated, is still in force under the the title "The Law of Land Warfare."[2] It is set forth therein that the laws of war are part of the law of the United States, and that they may be enforced against both soldiers and civilians, including enemy personnel, by general courts-martial, military commissions, or other military or international tribunals.

Comparable though not identical publications have been issued by the military authorities of Britain, France, Germany and many other countries. These documents, and the treaties on which they are largely based, are regarded as a comprehensive but not necessarily complete exposition of what is really a body of international common law—the laws of war.

Since the mid-19th century, with increasing frequency, the major powers have utilized military courts for the trial of persons accused of war crimes. An early and now famous trial, depicted in a suc-

cessful Broadway play, was the post-Civil War proceeding against the Confederate Major Henry Wirz
on charges of responsibility for the death of thousands of Union prisoners in the Andersonville prison
camp, of which he had been commandant. War
crimes tribunals were convened by the United
States after the Spanish-American War, and by the
British after the Boer War.

Following the defeat of Germany in the First
World War, the Allies demanded that nearly 900
Germans accused of war crimes, including military
and political leaders, be handed over for trial on war
crimes charges. The Germans resisted the demand,
and in the upshot they were allowed to try their
own "war criminals." The trials in 1921 and 1922
were not conducted by military courts, but by the
Supreme Court of Germany, sitting in Leipzig.
From the Allied standpoint they were a fiasco, as
only a handful of accused were tried, and of these
nearly all were acquitted or allowed to escape their
very short prison sentences. The German court did,
however, affirm that violations of the laws of war are
punishable offenses, and in the *Llandovery Castle*
case sentenced two German U-boat officers to four-
year prison terms (from which both soon escaped)
for complicity in the torpedoing of a British hospital
ship and the shelling and sinking of her life-boats.

Such was the state of development of the laws of
war, as the First World War faded into the pages
of history. Twenty years later, as the legions of the
Wehrmacht swarmed over Europe, putting the
monarchs and ministers of the German-occupied

nations to flight, London became the capital city of
the governments-in-exile. King Haakon of Norway,
Queen Wilhelmina of the Netherlands, Grand
Duchess Charlotte of Luxembourg, President Benes
of Czechoslovakia, the emigré ministers of Belgium
and Poland, and General Charles de Gaulle of the
Free French found British sanctuary in 1940, and
the next year were joined by King Peter of Yugoslavia and King Constantine of Greece.

London was not only the lodestone of the forces
bent on the liberation of Europe, but their listening-
post as well. By myriad means—clandestine radio
messages, reports of spies and couriers, dispatches
of neutral diplomats and churchmen—the British
and their refugee guests were informed of happen-
ings behind the coastal walls of Adolf Hitler's "For-
tress Europe," and the picture thus painted dark-
ened month by month.

Before the end of 1939, the press and radio of the
Vatican, on the high authority of August Cardinal
Hlond, the Primate of Poland, told their readers and
listeners that hundreds of Polish priests had been
executed by Heinrich Himmler's SS units. Early in
1940, the United States Embassy in Berlin transmit-
ted news of the wholesale deportation of German
Jews to Poland. In the wake of the Nazi conquest
of the western European countries in 1940, and of
Yugoslavia and Greece in 1941, came a flood of reports describing the round-up of millions of men
and women for forced labor in German mines and
factories, and occupational regimes of unexampled
severity, relying on the taking and frequent execution of hostages to maintain civil order. Soon after

the invasion of Russia, the Soviet authorities publicized captured German military orders declaring that the "supply of food to local inhabitants and prisoners of war is unnecessary humanitarianism," and calling for the most far-reaching confiscation of all things of value, down to children's boots. Russian prisoners of war in German hands froze and starved to death by the millions. And in 1942 came the first stories, at first incredible but soon confirmed, of the mass extermination of Jews from all the occupied countries at Auschwitz and other concentration camps in Poland—the holocaust described by the Nazis as the "final solution of the Jewish problem."

Thus horror was heaped on outrage, but what was to be done about it? On Oct. 25, 1941, in separate but simultaneous declarations, Winston Churchill and Franklin D. Roosevelt denounced the executions of hostages in France and other German-occupied countries. Soon other voices spoke more explicitly—those of the governments-in-exile in London. Representatives of these nine governments established an "Inter Allied Conference on the Punishment of War Crimes" which, on Jan. 13, 1942, promulgated what became known as the "Declaration of St. James." After making reference to the "regime of terror" instituted by Germany in their several countries, the signatories expressly repudiated the idea that the perpetrators of these atrocities could adequately be dealt with "by acts of vengeance on the part of the general public." On the contrary, it was declared that "the sense of justice of the civilized world" required that the signatory powers "place among their principal war aims the punishment through channels of organized justice, of those guilty of or responsible for these crimes."

The following year, with the announced support of the United States, Britain, and 15 other Allied governments, the "United Nations War Crimes Commission" was established in London. The Commission's main functions were to serve as a repository for evidence concerning war crimes, compile lists of individuals accused of their commission, and make plans for the apprehension and trial of those accused.

In the United States, as the defeat of Germany appeared more probable and imminent, the Judge Advocate General of the Army took the lead in preparations for war crimes trials at the conclusion of the war. Late in 1944 his activities were overshadowed by decisions at a higher level, which ultimately led to the establishment of the Nuremberg tribunals. As wo will see in a later chapter, most of the prominent Germans and Japanese accused of war crimes were tried at Nuremberg and Tokyo before courts established under international authority, and quite outside the usual channels of military justice.

But those channels remained open and, numerically, the Nuremberg and Tokyo trials were a small part of a very large picture. In Europe, the United States Army judge advocate was made responsible for the prosecution of crimes committed against American troops, or in Nazi concentration camps that had been overrun and "liberated" by American forces. Under this authority, some 1,600 German war crimes defendants (as compared with 200 at Nuremberg) were tried before Army military commissions

27

and military government courts, and over 250 death sentences (as compared with 21 at Nuremberg) were carried out. About an equal number were tried by British, French and other military courts established by the countries that had been occupied by Germany.

Precise figures are lacking, but by the spring of 1948 some 3,500 individuals had been tried on war crimes charges in Europe and 2,800 in the Far East, taking no account of trials held by the Soviet Union or China. It would be a conservative estimate that some 10,000 persons were tried on such charges from 1945 to 1950, and during the past 10 years hundreds more have been, and still are being, tried before West German courts. With a few exceptions, these trials were exclusively concerned with violations of the laws of war, and for the most part the charges related to mistreatment either of prisoners of war, or of the civilian populations of occupied countries.

We have looked back at a period of more than a hundred years since the laws of war began to emerge from their ancient form as unwritten rules of conduct, and to take shape in treaties, military manuals and the decisions of military courts established for their enforcement. Despite this century of development, as will be seen, the laws of war remain vague and uncertain in many respects. But a number of basic characteristics are by now manifest, and we should take note of them before examining the application of these laws to the fighting in Vietnam.

The first of these is that the laws of war remain

a body of what lawyers call "customary" laws—that is to say, laws that are not created by statutes enacted by legislatures, but develop from societal custom and practice. The reason is very simple: There is no international legislature, and thus no way to give the laws of war statutory form. The laws of war, like much other international law, have grown in somewhat the same manner that the common law of England grew in pre-Parliamentary times, and during the several centuries when very little of the basic civil and criminal law of England was to be found in Parliamentary statutes, but rather in the decisions of the English common-law courts—judge-made law based on custom and precedent.

Treaties such as The Hague and Geneva conventions, and military directives such as the Army field manual are not, therefore, the *sources* of the laws of war. Official directives may be binding as a matter of national law on the armed forces of the issuing country, and treaties may be binding on the signatory nations. But treaties and manuals alike are only partial embodiments of the laws of war on which they are based. This was clearly recognized in the preamble to the Fourth Hague Convention of 1907, by the statement that questions not covered by the Convention should be resolved by "the principles of the law of nations, as they result from the usages established among civilized peoples, from the laws of humanity, and from the dictates of the public conscience." Similar language is to be found in Article 158 of the Geneva Convention of 1949, "For the Protection of Civilian Persons in Time of War," where it is provided that a signatory nation may denounce the treaty, but will nevertheless remain bound to abide by the "principles of the law of nations," which are then described in the same words used in the Hague Convention.

For present purposes, the highly important consequence of all this is that nations are regarded as bound by the laws of war whether or not they are parties to The Hague and Geneva conventions. In fact, not all countries have signed those treaties, and nonsigning countries have sometimes declared that they would nevertheless agree to observe them, and sometimes have said the opposite, or nothing at all. Nonsignatory nations are, to be sure, not bound by the precise wording and detailed prescriptions of the treaties, but, as the 1949 Geneva Convention expressly provides, they are bound by the customary laws of war from which the treaties are derived.

Of course, the reference in the Hague Convention preamble to "civilized" nations suggests what is obvious: that savage tribes may not be held to standards of conduct wholly unfamiliar to them. But the days of Custer and Kipling are over, and in the true tales of those years the colonial soldier comes off little better than the savage. Whether today we are all civilized or all barbarians, the distinction is no longer of much importance so far as concerns the applicability of the laws of war.

A second and very basic characteristic of the laws of war and war crimes is that, as these names indicate, they concern only conduct which is directly related to *war*—to hostilities in progress between organized belligerent forces. When the Nazis killed or assaulted German Jews in Germany, that may have been a crime, but it was not a war crime. At Nuremberg, an effort was made to give such domestic atrocities international significance under the expression "crimes against humanity," and today they would no doubt be covered by the international treaty defining and condemning "genocide," which most nations (not including the United States) have signed. "Genocide" and "crimes against humanity" will be pertinent to the discussion at a later point, but clarity requires that they be distinguished from the "war crimes" with which we are presently concerned.

This does not mean that a war that brings the laws of war into effect must be an international war. It may be a civil war; as we have seen, it was during our own War Between the States that the first effort to codify the laws of war was made. But traditional war crimes involve the belligerent relation —between the armed forces of the hostile parties, or between armed forces and the civilian population of the enemy country.* The coverage of the Geneva

---

\* It is interesting to note that while most violations of the laws of war consist of homicidal or other acts involving moral obloquy, this is not universally true, even with respect to conduct capitally punishable. A good example is spying. Of course, if one spies against one's own country, then traitorous or even treasonable elements are present. But spying for one's country, though punishable by death under the laws of war (explicitly recognized in Article 68 of the 1949 Geneva Convention on the protection of civilians), is not regarded as ignoble. We think of Major André as a blameless, luckless victim of Benedict Arnold's perfidy, and Nathan Hale is honored with a statue on the Old Campus at Yale and a plaque on the outside wall of the Yale Club in New York City, near where he was hanged by the British in 1776. That spying is not intrinsically criminal is interestingly recognized in Article 31 of the 1907 Hague Convention, which provides that a spy "who, after rejoining the army to which he belongs, is subsequently captured by the enemy, is treated as a prisoner of war and incurs no responsibility for his previous acts of espionage." Thus deterrence of others, not retribution or condemnation, is the object of capital punishment for spies caught in the act.

31

Conventions as amended in 1949 is considerably broader, and extends to all persons "in the hands of" a belligerent or occupying nation of which the persons are not nationals. In Vietnam, where the American forces are operating primarily on the territory of a presumptive ally (South Vietnam), the question whether or not the laws of war are applicable to a given situation may present considerable difficulties.

By now, the reader will surely understand that the laws of war, although a long-established reality with a substantial core of recognized practice, are very fuzzy around the edges. They are also, as we will now see, unstable in the sense that their enforcement is and has always been spasmodic and uneven, and changeable in that the extent to which they are observed may be rapidly altered by the circumstances and techniques of warfare.

In part this is due to the customary nature of the laws of war, and the lack of any authoritative source or means of systematic enforcement. For want of an international legislature, there is no single, authoritative text of the rules, and there are no prescribed penalties for their violation. In the rare instances, such as the Second World War, where hostilities end in total victory for one side, there may be extensive enforcement by the victorious powers against the vanquished. Otherwise, enforcement is limited to proceedings against prisoners of war, or against the enforcing power's own troops. In such an embryonic legislative and judicial context, it is hardly surprising that the effective content of the laws of war should fluctuate.

Even more, however, this amorphous, shifting quality of the laws of war is due to the nature of war itself. Otherwise law-abiding individuals will commit crimes in order to save their own lives; national governments will likewise break treaties and international rules, if necessary, for their own preservation. Intrinsically a desperate and violent business, war is not readily limitable in terms of the means to be used in its prosecution. Especially in modern times, war is a rapid breeder of new techniques, the successful use of or defense against which may be incompatible with the continued observance of rules previously respected.

These characteristics of warfare are epitomized in the expression "military necessity." The men who first undertook to give written form to the laws of war were acutely conscious of the bearing of this principle on the task they undertook. In the Lieber rules of 1863, military necessity was defined as "those measures which are indispensable for securing the ends of war, and which are lawful according to the modern law and usages of war."

This definition, neatly if unintentionally, reveals the great dilemma, as yet unresolved, that permeates the very concept of "laws of war." Is there any measure that by assumption is "indispensable for securing the ends of war" that the laws of war can effectively condemn? Or must we not accept Lowes Dickinson's flat verdict that "no rules to restrain the conduct of war will ever be observed if victory seems to depend upon the breach of them"?[3]

It is interesting to compare what was said about this problem in the Army's field manuals of 1917 and 1956. The earlier version declared that the laws of war were "determined by those principles," as follows:

> First, *that a belligerent is justified in applying any amount and any kind of force which is necessary for the purpose of the war; that is, the complete submission of the enemy at the earliest possible moment with the least expenditure of men and money.* Second, *the principle of humanity, which says that all such kinds and degrees of violence as are not necessary for the purpose of war are not permitted to a belligerent.* Third, *the principle of chivalry, which demands a certain amount of fairness in offense and defense and a certain mutual respect between opposing forces.*[4]

Except for the surpassingly vague "principle of chivalry," this is a plain statement of the rule of military necessity; if the use of force is necessary, it is lawful, and if unnecessary, it is unlawful. The 1940 manual was not significantly different, but in the most recent (1956) edition the matter is not at all so clear:

> *The law of war places limits on the exercise of a belligerent's power . . . and requires that belligerents refrain from employing any kind or degree of violence which is not actually necessary for military purposes and that they conduct hostilities with regard for the principles of humanity and chivalry.*
>
> *The prohibitory effect of the law of war is not minimized by "military necessity" which has been defined as that principle which justi-*

*fies those measures not forbidden by interna-*
*tional law which are indispensable for securing*
*the complete submission of the enemy as soon*
*as possible. Military necessity has been gener-*
*ally rejected as a defense for acts forbidden by*
*the customary and conventional laws of war*
*inasmuch as the latter have been developed*
*and framed with consideration for the concept*
*of military necessity.*[5]

The later statement surely rings less harshly in
the ear, but careful reading only heightens its ambiguity. In any event, no form of words can resolve
the essential difficulty, which is that "necessity" is
a matter of infinite circumstantial variation. To
illustrate the problem in the pragmatic dimension,
two examples may be helpful.

Perhaps the most important of all the laws of war
is the rule that an enemy soldier who surrenders is
to be spared further attack and, upon being taken
prisoner, is to be conducted, as soon as possible, to
safety in the rear of the capturing force. It is "especially forbidden" under the 1907 Hague Convention
"to kill or wound an enemy who, having laid down
his arms, or having no longer means of self-defence,
has surrendered at discretion." It is equally forbidden "to declare that no quarter will be given." And
under the 1949 Geneva Convention on prisoners of
war, they "shall be evacuated, as soon as possible
after their capture, to camps situated far enough
from the combat zone for them to be out of danger."

Now, these requirements are followed more often

than not, and for that reason millions are alive today who would otherwise be dead. But they are not infrequently violated; the rules read like absolute requirements, but circumstances arise where military necessity, or even something less, causes them to be disregarded. In the heat of combat, soldiers who are frightened, angered, shocked at the death of comrades, and fearful of treacherous attacks by enemies feigning death or surrender, are often prone to kill rather than capture. Under quite different circumstances, the killing may be done in cold blood, by order of humane commanders. Small detachments on special missions, or accidentally cut off from their main force, may take prisoners under such circumstances that men cannot be spared to guard them or take them to the rear, and that to take them along would greatly endanger the success of the mission or the safety of the unit. The prisoners will be killed, by operation of the principle of military necessity,* and no military or other court has been called upon, so far as I am aware, to declare such killing a war crime.

An equally striking illustration of the "necessity" principle may be drawn from the development of submarine warfare. During the First World War, the havoc worked by German U-boats in sinking merchant and passenger vessels (notably the *Lusitania*) led to strong pressure, especially from neutral nations, to limit their depredations. A conse-

---

* The Lieber rules of 1863 recognized this necessity by providing that "a commander is permitted to direct his troops to give no quarter, in great straits, when his own salvation makes it *impossible* to cumber himself with prisoners." The Hague and Geneva Rules and the recent Army Manuals contain no comparable provision.

quence of these widely held sentiments was the provision of the London Naval Treaty of 1930, subsequently agreed to by the United States, France, Italy, Japan, Great Britain and Germany, forbidding warships "whether surface or submarine" from sinking merchant vessels "without having first placed passengers, crew, and ship's papers in a place of safety."

Soon after the outbreak of the Second World War, it became apparent that submarine operations could no longer be effectively conducted (if indeed they ever could have been) in accordance with these rescue requirements. Radar, sonar, convoys and long-range aircraft rapidly advanced the techniques of antisubmarine warfare to such a point that it was virtual suicide for a submarine to surface anywhere near its target, let alone to remain in the vicinity for rescue operations. During the war the German, British and American submarine forces all disregarded the rescue provisions of the London treaty.

Nevertheless, at Nuremberg Admirals Erich Raeder and Karl Doenitz, successively Commanders-in-Chief of the German Navy, were charged with war crimes in that they were responsible for U-boat operations in violation of the London treaty. But the evidence at the trial, which included testimony by the American naval commander in the Pacific, Admiral Chester W. Nimitz, established that in this regard the Germans had done nothing that the British and Americans had not also done. The Nuremberg tribunal therefore ruled that, while Raeder and Doenitz had indeed violated the London rescue stipulations, they should not be subjected to any criminal penalties on that account. The plain rationale of this decision was that the London rescue requirements were no longer an effective part of the laws of naval warfare, because they had been abrogated by the practice of the belligerents on both sides under the stress of military necessity.

Other examples of the impact of military necessity on the laws of war come readily to mind. A signal and terrible example during the Second World War was the growing acceptance of aerial bombardment of population centers—from the prewar Japanese and German attacks on Canton and Barcelona, through London, Coventry, Belgrade, Hamburg and Berlin, to Dresden, Tokyo, Hiroshima and Nagasaki in 1945. On this matter there will be more to say in relation to Vietnam. I mention it here to underline the lesson of all these examples, which is that the laws of war do not have a fixed content, but are constantly reshaped by the exigencies of warfare.

To be sure, there is abundant room for the view that the laws of war should be closer to fixed principles of conduct, less at the mercy of military pressures. If there were an international criminal tribunal, with jurisdiction over all nations, it might then be possible to ban specific weapons or practices as inhumane and unlawful, regardless of their military value. Perhaps one day there will be such a court, but its creation would hardly be possible except in a climate of world opinion in which war itself could be eliminated.

But as long as enforcement of the laws of war

is left to the belligerents themselves, whether during the course of hostilities or by the victors at their conclusion, the scope of their application must be limited by the extent to which they have been observed by the enforcing party. To punish the foe —especially the vanquished foe—for conduct in which the enforcing nation has engaged, would be so grossly inequitable as to discredit the laws themselves.

If, then, the laws of war are so erratically if not capriciously enforced, and subject to change under the pressure of military practice, are they worth having at all? Might it not be better to junk the whole concept of war crimes, and acknowledge that war is war and anything goes? Indeed, if warring nations were totally uninhibited, might not the very enormity of the consequences revolt the conscience of the world and lend additional strength to the movement for abolition of war?

Support for affirmative answers to these questions has not been lacking, and is perhaps more extensive than the literature on the subject suggests. But such views are, I believe, counsels of desperation with little in logic or experience to commend them. All in all this has been a pretty bloody century and people do not seem to shock very easily, as much of the popular reaction to the reports of Son My made depressingly plain. The kind of world in which all efforts to mitigate the horrors of war are abandoned would hardly be a world sensitive to the consequences.

There are at least two reasons—or perhaps one

basic reason with two formulations—for the preservation and continued enforcement, as even-handedly as possible, of the laws of war. The first is strictly pragmatic: They work. Violated or ignored as they often are, enough of the rules are observed enough of the time so that mankind is very much better off with them than without them. The rules for the treatment of civilian populations in occupied countries are not as susceptible to technological change as rules regarding the use of weapons in combat. If it were not regarded as wrong to bomb military hospitals, they would be bombed all of the time instead of some of the time.

It is only necessary to consider the rules on taking prisoners in the setting of the Second World War to realize the enormous saving of life for which they have been responsible. Millions of French, British, German and Italian soldiers captured in Western Europe and Africa were treated in general compliance with The Hague and Geneva requirements, and returned home at the end of the war. German and Russian prisoners taken on the eastern front did not fare nearly so well and died in captivity by the millions, but many survived. Today there is surely much to criticize about the handling of prisoners on both sides of the Vietnam war, but at least many of them are alive, and that is because the belligerents are reluctant to flout the laws of war too openly.

Another and, to my mind, even more important basis of the laws of war is that they are necessary to diminish the corrosive effect of mortal combat on the participants. War does not confer a license to kill for personal reasons—to gratify perverse impulses, or to put out of the way anyone who appears obnoxious, or to whose welfare the soldier is indifferent. War is not a license at all, but an obligation to kill for reasons of state; it does not countenance the infliction of suffering for its own sake or for revenge.

Unless troops are trained and required to draw the distinction between military and nonmilitary killings, and to retain such respect for the value of life that unnecessary death and destruction will continue to repel them, they may lose the sense for that distinction for the rest of their lives. The consequence would be that many returning soldiers would be potential murderers.

As Francis Lieber put the matter in his 1863 Army regulations: "Men who take up arms against one another in public war do not cease on this account to be moral beings, responsible to one another and to God."

# 2/Superior Orders and Reprisals

MORAL RESPONSIBILITY is all very well, the reader may be thinking, but what about military orders? Is it not the soldier's first duty to give instant obedience to orders given by his military superiors? And apart from duty, will not the soldier suffer severe punishment, even death, if he refuses to do what he is ordered to do? If, then, a soldier is told by his sergeant or lieutenant to burn this house or shoot that prisoner, how can he be held criminally accountable on the ground that the burning or shooting was a violation of the laws of war?

These are some of the questions that are raised by the concept commonly called "superior orders," and its use as a defense in war crimes trials. It is an issue that must be as old as the laws of war themselves, and it emerged in legal guise over three centuries ago when, after the Stuart restoration in 1660, the commander of the guards at the trial and execution of Charles I was put on trial for treason and murder. The officer defended himself on the ground "that all he did was as a soldier, by the command of his superior officer whom he must obey or die," but the court gave him short shrift, saying that "when the command is traitorous, then the obedience to that command is also traitorous."[1]

Though not precisely articulated, the rule that is necessarily implied by this decision is that it is the soldier's duty to obey *lawful* orders, but that he may disobey—and indeed must, under some circumstances—unlawful orders. Such has been the law of the United States since the birth of the nation. In 1804, Chief Justice John Marshall declared that superior orders will justify a subordinate's conduct only "if not to perform a prohibited act," and there are many other early decisions to the same effect.[2]

A strikingly illustrative case occurred in the wake of that conflict of which most Englishmen have never heard (although their troops burned the White House) and which we call the War of 1812. Our country was badly split by that war too and, at a time when the United States Navy was not especially popular in New England, the ship-of-the-line *Independence* was lying in Boston Harbor. A passer-by directed abusive language at a marine standing guard on the ship, and the marine, Bevans by name, ran his bayonet through the man. Charged with murder, Bevans produced evidence that the marines on the *Independence* had been ordered to bayonet anyone showing them disrespect. The case was tried before Justice Joseph Story, next to Marshall the leading judicial figure of those years, who charged the jury that any such order as Bevans had invoked "would be illegal and void," and if given and put into practice, both superior and subordinate would be guilty of murder. In consequence, Bevans was convicted.[3]

The order allegedly given to Bevans was pretty drastic, and Boston Harbor was not a battlefield; perhaps it was not too much to expect the marine to realize that literal compliance might lead to bad trouble. But it is only too easy to conceive of circumstances where the matter might not be at all clear. Does the subordinate obey at peril that the order may later be ruled illegal, or is he protected unless he had good reason to doubt its validity?

The early cases did not answer this question uniformly or precisely. There are rigid, absolute formulations, such as the statement of Chief Justice Taney in 1851 that: "It can never be maintained that a military officer can justify himself for doing an unlawful act, by producing the order of his superior."[4] More realistic judicial assessments, however, recognized that often the subordinate is in no position to determine the legality or illegality of the order, and that the very nature of military service requires prompt obedience. "While subordinate officers are pausing to consider whether they ought to obey, or are scrupulously weighing the evidence of the facts upon which the commander-in-chief exercises the right to demand their services," Justice Story observed in 1827, "the hostile enterprise may be accomplished." Twenty-five years later Justice Curtis made much the same point in a case where the soldier was sued for false arrest: "I do not think the defendant was bound to go behind the order, apparently lawful, and satisfy himself by inquiry that his commanding officer proceeded upon sufficient grounds. To require this would be destructive of military discipline and of the necessary promptness and efficiency of the service."[5]

Much the most dramatic case in American military history which turned on this problem was the trial, already mentioned, of Major Henry Wirz, the commandant of the Confederate prison camp at Andersonville, Ga. Abundant and virtually uncontested evidence showed that the Union prisoners were herded into a camp altogether lacking shelter, so that they froze in winter and burned in summer; that the stream constituting the sole source of water was constantly fouled by corpses and human waste; that the food was totally inadequate, despite abundant harvests in the country around the camp; that neighboring farmers, hearing of the starvation rampant at the camp, came with wagonloads of food for their relief, but were turned away by Wirz; that the camp was a nightmare of hunger, exposure and disease and that the inmates died at the rate of several hundred a week, mounting to a total of some 14,000 by the end of the war.[6]

Wirz was tried before a military commission of six Union generals and two colonels, presided over by Major General Lew Wallace, a minor but protean historical figure who, apart from his military exploits, was a politician, diplomat, lawyer, and author of the fabulously successful novel "Ben-Hur." A rigid-minded German Swiss, Wirz defended himself on the ground that his administration of the camp was governed by orders from General John H. Winder, the officer in charge of all Confederate prison camps. The evidence bore out his claim, but the prosecution took the position that Wirz had followed orders willingly rather than under duress, and that Wirz and Winder were co-conspirators. The military commission found Wirz guilty of both conspiring to destroy the lives of Union soldiers and of murder "in violation of the laws and customs of war," and sentenced him to be hanged. Presumably, therefore, it must have accepted the prosecution's contention, though (in accordance with the practice of military courts) there was no written opinion.*

Awareness that a problem is an old one is not, of course, the key to its solution. But these cases of many years past are important, I believe, in showing that the idea that under some circumstances military orders ought to be disobeyed is not a novel doctrine first conceived at Nuremberg. Furthermore, while the earliest decisions on the point were rendered by civilian judges, the modern development of the doctrine during the 75 years following

---

* In the play based on the trial, Wirz's last line is, "I did not have that feeling of strength to do that. I could not disobey." There is an interesting likeness between this language and the statement of the German Supreme Court in the *Llandovery Castle* case (convicting two naval lieutenants who had acted under superior orders) that: "A refusal to obey the commander of a submarine would have been something so unusual, that it is humanly possible to understand that the accused could not bring themselves to disobey."

the Civil War was largely the work of military men.

The Lieber regulations and The Hague and Geneva conventions are silent on this subject, and the earliest statement of a general, governing rule appeared in the German Military Penal Code of 1872, Article 47 of which provided:

> *If execution of an order given in line of duty violates a statute of the penal code, the superior giving the order is alone responsible. However, the subordinate obeying the order is liable to punishment as an accomplice if . . . he knew that the order involved an act the commission of which constituted a civil or military crime or offense.*

The imposition of responsibility on those giving illegal orders, but not the secondary responsibility of subordinates who carry out orders known to be illegal, was provided for in the British and American Army manuals published in 1914.[7] Both explicitly exempted from liability those whose violations of the laws of war were committed under orders of their "government" or "commanders," while declaring that the commanders who ordered or authorized the offenses might be punished. These provisions raised questions whether anyone at all could be held liable if the "commanders" were themselves acting under orders from still farther up the military chain of command.

At the outbreak of the Second World War, accordingly, military law on the question of superior orders was in a state of considerable confusion. The British and American manuals appeared to treat them as an absolute defense to charges against an accused subordinate, but was this really intended, no matter how atrocious the order? Perhaps not, for elsewhere the British manual called for "prompt, immediate, and unhesitating obedience" only when the "orders of the superior are not obviously and decidedly in opposition to the law of the land or to the well-known and established customs of the army." The German law of 1872 embodied a more rational approach and, despite all the horrors of the Nazi conquests and exterminations, it remained in effect throughout the war, and was reaffirmed in principle by no less a person than Dr. Joseph Goebbels, the Minister of Propaganda, who in May, 1944, published an article condemning Allied bombing operations, in which he declared:

> No international law of warfare is in existence which provides that a soldier who has committed a mean crime can escape punishment by pleading as his defence that he followed the commands of his superiors. This holds particularly true if those commands are contrary to all human ethics and opposed to the well-established usage of warfare.[8]

During the same year (1944) the British and American military establishments revised the "superior orders" provisions of their field manuals.[9] The new British language adopted the essential principle of the German law of 1872, cast in discursive rather than statutory terms. Members of the armed forces "are bound to obey lawful orders only"; to be sure, in conditions of "war discipline" they could not "be expected to weigh scrupulously the legal merits of the order received," but they could not "escape liability if, in obedience to a command, they commit acts which both violate unchallenged rules of warfare and outrage the general sentiment of humanity."

The 1944 American provision was quite different, for it stated no guiding principle whatever. Individuals who violate the laws of war "may be punished therefor," it declared, adding: "However, the fact that the acts complained of were done pursuant to order of a superior or government sanction may be taken into consideration in determining culpability, either by way of defence or in mitigation of punishment." But *when* should such orders "be taken into consideration," and what should determine whether the orders ought to be considered as a defense or merely in mitigation? It was a most unsatisfactory formulation.

Scrutiny of these efforts of military men to grapple with the effect of superior orders, as a defense to war crimes charges, discloses that the problem involves two quite different factors, one of which is appropriate by way of defense, and the other only in mitigation. The first is essentially a question of *knowledge*, and the second a question of *fear*.

Some orders are so atrocious, or plainly unlawful, that the subordinate must know, or can reasonably be held to know, that they should not be obeyed. But, especially in combat situations, there are bound to be many orders the legitimacy of which depends on the prevailing circumstances, the existence and sufficiency of which will be beyond the reach of the subordinate's observation or judgment. The military service is based on obedience to orders passed down through the chain of command, and the success of military operations often depends on the speed and precision with which orders are executed. Especially in the lower ranks, virtually unquestioning obedience to orders, other than those that are palpably vicious, is a necessary feature of military life. If the subordinate is expected to give such obedience, he should also be entitled to rely on the order as a full and complete defense to any charge that his act was unlawful. The German law of 1872 was therefore rightly conceived insofar as it made the subordinate's liability turn on his awareness of the order's unlawful quality.

But knowledge is not the end of the problem. Suppose the soldier is indeed aware that the order is beyond the pale, but is confronted by a superior who is backing his command with threat of stern punishment, perhaps immediate death. It is one thing to require men at war to risk their lives against the enemy, but quite another to expect them to face severe or even capital penalties on the basis of their own determination that their superior's command is unlawful. Such a course calls for a high degree of moral as well as physical courage; men are not to be judged too severely for falling short, and mitigation of the punishment is appropriate.

Substantially these rules—that lack of knowledge of an order's unlawfulness is a defense, and fear of punishment for disobedience a mitigating circumstance—are embodied in the Army's current field manual, issued in 1956:

*a. The fact that the law of war has been violated pursuant to an order of a superior authority, whether military or civil, does not deprive the act in question of its character of a war crime, nor does it constitute a defense in the trial of an accused individual, unless he did not know and could not reasonably have been expected to know that the act ordered was unlawful. In all cases where the order is held not to constitute a defense to an allegation of war crime, the fact that the individual was acting pursuant to orders may be considered in mitigation of punishment.*

*b. In considering the question whether a superior order constitutes a valid defense, the court shall take into consideration the fact that obedience to lawful military orders is the duty of every member of the armed forces; that the latter cannot be expected, in conditions of war discipline, to weigh scrupulously the legal merits of the orders received; that certain rules of warfare may be controversial; or that an act otherwise amounting to a war crime may be done in obedience to orders conceived as a measure of reprisal. At the same time it must be borne in mind that members of the armed forces are bound to obey only lawful orders.*[10]

These principles are sound, and the language is well chosen to convey the quality of the factors, imponderable as they are, that must be assessed in a given case. As with so many good rules, the difficulty lies in its application—in weighing evidence that is likely to be ambiguous or conflicting. Was

there a superior order? Especially at the lower
levels, many orders are given orally. Was a particular remark or look intended as an order, and if so
what was its scope? If the existence and meaning
of the order are reasonably clear, there may still be
much doubt about the attendant circumstances—
how far the obeying soldier was aware of them, and
how well equipped to judge them. If the order was
plainly illegal, to what degree of duress was the
subordinate subjected? Especially in confused
ground fighting of the type prevalent in Vietnam,
evidentiary questions such as these may be extremely difficult to resolve.

The doctrine of "superior orders" as a defense for
the subordinate is, of course, the converse of what
lawyers call *respondeat superior*—the liability of the
order-giver. And in conclusion, it should be emphasized that the consequence of allowing superior
orders as a defense is not to eliminate criminal responsibility for what happened, but to shift its
locus upwards. It would stultify the whole system
to exculpate the underlings who follow orders and
ignore the superiors who give them. Indeed, the
greater the indulgence shown to the soldier on the
theory that his first duty is to give unquestioning
obedience, the greater the responsibility of the officer to see to it that obedience entails no criminal
consequences.

The superior's responsibility, moreover, is not limited to the situation where he has given affirmative
orders. A commander is responsible for the conduct
of his troops, and is expected to take all necessary
action to see that they do not, on their own initia-

tive, commit war crimes. Gen. George B. McClellan, as commander of the Army of the Potomac in 1861, warned all of his officers that they would "be held responsible for punishing aggression by those under their command," and directed that military commissions be established to punish any persons connected with his Army who might engage in conduct "in contravention of the established rules of law." The 1956 Army Manual provides explicitly that a military commander is responsible not only for criminal acts committed in pursuance of his orders, but "is also responsible if he has actual knowledge, or should have knowledge . . . that troops or other persons subject to his control are about to commit or have committed a war crime and he fails to take the necessary and reasonable steps to insure compliance with the law of war or to punish violations thereof."[11]

This language embodied no novel conception of a commander's responsibility. Ten years earlier, a military commission of American generals condemned General Tomayuki Yamashita to death by hanging, for failure properly to control the conduct of Japanese troops under his command in the Philippines. The *Yamashita* case, and the principles that it exemplifies, are of great importance in establishing the reach of criminal responsibility for episodes such as those said to have occurred at Son My.

Another doctrine, which may be invoked to justify conduct that otherwise would be a war crime, is that of *reprisals*. Today the open resort to reprisals is not as frequent as in earlier times, but the concept is nonetheless of great importance in relation to the conduct of the war in Vietnam.

In origin, a reprisal (or "retaliation," as Lieber called it) was an action taken by a nation against an enemy that would normally be a violation of the laws of war, but that was justified as necessary to prevent the enemy from continuing to violate the laws of war. Thus if one side makes a practice of shooting medical corpsmen or bombing hospitals, the other side may take action by way of reprisal in order to dissuade the enemy from continuing his unlawful course of conduct. The justification for reprisals was the lack of any apparent alternative; the enemy miscreants were beyond the reach of the offended belligerent, and protests had proved fruitless. As Lieber put it, their purpose was not "mere revenge," but rather "protective retribution."

Resort to reprisals in order to bring an enemy government back to the paths of military virtue is still recognized by the laws of war, subject to various restrictions written into the Geneva Conventions and the recent army field manuals. But reprisals of this type are not much used today, partly because they are generally ineffective, and partly because the resort to crime in order to reform the criminal is an unappetizing method. Generally, a nation that deliberately embarks on a course of conduct violative of the laws of war will have taken into account the possibility and effect of reprisals, and will not be easily checked. Then crime and reprisal both continue, and the standards of warfare are debased.

But reprisals of another type, directed not against an enemy government but against the civilian population of territory under military occupation, are of great significance in relation to both Nuremberg and the Vietnam war. They were inflicted on a number of occasions during the Civil War,* and used extensively by the Germans during the Franco-Prussian War of 1871 and the First World War. One example from many is General Karl von Bülow's proclamation of Aug. 22, 1914, issued in the course of the German advance into Belgium:

> The inhabitants of the town of Andenne, after having protested their peaceful intentions, made a treacherous surprise attack on our troops.
>
> It was with my consent that the General had the whole place burned down, and about one hundred people shot.
>
> I bring this fact to the attention of the town of Liège, so that its inhabitants may know the fate with which they are threatened, if they take a similar attitude.

Closely related to the matter of reprisals is the practice of taking hostages. In past centuries, two countries that had made a treaty often exchanged

---

* In 1864, the Union General David Hunter burned many Virginia homes during his advance in the Shenandoah Valley. The Confederate General Jubal Early drove Hunter's forces back across the Potomac and, when Confederate troops reached Chambersburg, Pa., Early ordered the town burned by way of reprisal. The regimental commander in Chambersburg, Colonel William E. Peters, refused to obey Early's order, and was relieved of his command and placed under arrest, while others did the burning. There is a vivid account of all this in the Confederate General John B. Gordon's "Reminiscences of the Civil War" (1903), in which the author pays high tribute to Peters's courage and chivalry, and states that "prudently and wisely, he was never brought to trial for his disobedience."

hostages, as mutual security for compliance. In modern warfare, civilian hostages have been taken by armies occupying enemy territory, as a measure of ensuring the good behavior of the local population.

Before the Second World War, the state of the laws of war with respect to the use of reprisals and the taking and treatment of hostages in occupied territory was one of considerable confusion and conflict. The American field manuals of 1914 and 1940, perhaps influenced by the Army's experience in the "pacification" of the Philippines after the Spanish-American War, gave the occupying power great latitude for positive action. The 1940 manual included the following:

> *Hostages taken and held for the declared purpose of insuring against unlawful acts by the enemy forces or people may be punished or put to death if the unlawful acts are nevertheless committed. . . . Villages or houses, etc., may be burned for acts of hostility committed from them, where the guilty individuals cannot be identified, tried and punished. Collective punishments may be inflicted either in the form of fines or otherwise.*[12]

To what extent such language reflected international opinion on the point is hard to say. Draconic as it is, the American provision would have fallen far short of authorizing the extensive and ruthless use of hostages and reprisals that characterized the German military regimes in the occupied countries of Europe, especially in the Balkans and Russia. In consequence, these problems were an important part of the subject matter of the Nuremberg trials, as will shortly appear.

After Nuremberg, hostages and reprisal questions were considered in framing the 1949 Geneva Convention Relative to the Protection of Civilian Persons in Time of War, and important reforms were adopted, which were carried into the 1956 Army manual. Under these new provisions, the taking of hostages is entirely forbidden, and the permissible scope of reprisals is much more restricted than it was under the 1940 manual.

The trend of the laws of war since the Second World War is in line with Francis Lieber's judgment, expressed in the 1863 rules, that: "Unjust or inconsiderate retaliation removes the belligerents farther and farther from the mitigating rules of regular warfare, and by rapid steps leads them nearer to the internecine wars of savages."

# 3/Just and Unjust Wars

OVER THE CENTURIES of recorded history, warfare has shown a remarkable and, to most of us, a distressing vitality as a staple ingredient of intercourse among families and tribes at first, and then peoples, religions and nations. No doubt a continuing pessimism about the likelihood that war can be abolished has lent force to men's efforts to confine wars and limit their methods and effects, as described in the previous chapters.

Throughout these same centuries, however, war has been practiced against a counterpoint of belief that as a destroyer of man and men's works, war is evil—an insult to human dignity, and a peril to humanity's capacity to develop or, indeed, to survive. Since the early civilizations men have speculated about ways of eliminating war, and since the middle ages one of those ways has been the enunciation of rules of conduct, which gradually assumed the characteristics of law.

The laws of war have been developed largely by men who fought in them—military men. The principles concerning the moral or legal legitimacy of war itself, on the other hand, have been the work of theologians, jurists, and in more recent years, of diplomats. It was St. Augustine of Hippo (A.D. 354–430) who first enunciated the doctrine of "just and unjust wars," and two ministers for foreign affairs, Frank B. Kellogg of the United States and Aristide Briand of France, whose names are attached to the 1928 Pact of Paris, which condemned "recourse to war for the solution of international controversies."

The Master, as far as we know, had little to say about war or international relations; He was not a nationalist ("My Kingdom is not of this world") nor a political revolutionary ("Render to Caesar the things that are Caesar's"). But in the Gospels there is much emphasis on nonresistance and forgiveness of enemies, and during the first three centuries after Christ there grew up among His followers a strong school of religious pacifism. Furthermore, the early Christians were a religious minority in a pagan state, and the higher ranks of the Roman military service were required to offer sacrifice to the Emperor—an act of idolatry which was anathema to Christians. For these reasons Tertullian, Origen and other fathers of the Church condemned all military service as incompatible with the Christian life.

But there were those who thought otherwise, and

in fact there were many Christians in the Roman soldiery. The Emperor Constantine's official toleration of Christianity (A.D. 312) and death-bed conversion (A.D. 337) foreshadowed a great change in the Christian attitude toward war: "A Christian empire and a Christian army defending the nucleus of the civilized world against heretics and vandals created an atmosphere more favorable to the conception of a holy war waged by a Chosen People than did a pagan empire persecuting a Christian minority." In this state of doctrinal flux, St. Augustine emerged as "the great co-ordinator of Christian doctrine upon peace and war."[1]

He accomplished this by drawing a distinction between "just and unjust wars," a vocabulary that was not new, but that the Saint applied by reference to general ethical standards rather than the ambitions of rulers. The Roman wars of conquest he did not hesitate to condemn: "To make war on your neighbors, and thence to proceed to others, and through mere lust of dominion to crush and subdue people who do you no harm, what else is this to be called than robbery on a grand scale?" He praised as "elegant and excellent" the pirate's reply to Alexander the Great, who had asked how he dared molest the seas: "Because I do it with a little ship only, I am called a thief; thou, doing it with a great navy, art called an emperor." On the other hand, it was wholly possible "to please God while engaged in military service." Just wars, according to Augustine, "are usually defined as those which avenge injuries, when the nation or city against which warlike action is to be directed has neglected to punish wrongs committed by its own citizens, or to restore what has been unjustly taken by it." Indeed, the true aim of a just war is peace, so that "after the resisting nations have been conquered, provision may more easily be made for enjoying in peace the mutual bond of piety and justice."

Augustine's tenets were approved and elaborated by the medieval theologians, most notably by St. Thomas Aquinas (1225–1274) in his *Summa Theologiae*. "In order that a war may be just," he wrote, "three things are necessary":

> *In the first place, the authority of the prince, by whose order the war is undertaken; for it does not belong to a private individual to make war, because, in order to obtain justice he can have recourse to the judgment of his superior. . . . But, since the care of the State is confided to princes . . . it is to them that it belongs to bear the sword in combats for the defence of the State against external enemies . . .*
>
> *In the second place, there must be a just cause; that is to say, those attacked must, by a fault, deserve to be attacked . . .*
>
> *In the third place, it is necessary that the intention of those who fight should be right; that is to say, that they propose to themselves a good to be effected or an evil to be avoided . . . those who wage wars justly have peace as the object of their intention . . .*

The Augustinian and Thomist teachings have remained the core of Catholic doctrine on the rightfulness of war. It is really a matter of necessity; if there were a higher mundane power to order disputes among nations, as there is for individuals, there would be no basis for war. Lacking any other arbitrament, resort may be had to war if the cause is just. On what constitutes a just war, Aquinas added little to Augustine, but stressed the importance of a pure motive; one who has been injured may not exploit his just grievance as an opportunity to gratify a lust for revenge.

How the "justness" of a war should be determined was examined more closely in the 16th and 17th centuries by the great Spanish theologians Francisco de Vitoria (1480–1546), a Dominican, and Francisco Suarez (1548–1617), a Jesuit. Vitoria became concerned about the application of the "just war" principles to the Spanish conquests in the New World. Very much an "establishment" figure, Vitoria vindicated the Spanish Government's policies, but the strength of the Indians' right of self-defense must have impressed him, for his works lay great emphasis on the care that rulers should exercise before judging a prospective war to be "just." A mistake "would bring great evil and ruin to multitudes"; therefore "the reasons of those who on grounds of equity oppose the war ought to be listened to," and the final decision made only on the judgment "of many, and they wise and upright men."

Suarez's approach to these questions is much more legal and remarkably modern. The right of Christian rulers to make war, he declares, must have "at least some relation to the natural law"; that being so, it is not solely a Christian prerogative, and must also "suffice in some manner for non-Christian rulers." Defensive war is always legitimate, and may be a duty; this is as true between nations as between private individuals, for "the right of self-defence is a natural and necessary one." This sort of analogy he used as the basis for a triad of situations that would justify war: defense of life, defense of property and aid to a third party who is unjustly attacked. Thus the parallel between domestic and international criminal principles was articulated by a Spanish cleric three centuries before the efforts of recent years to define "aggressive war."

But the long reign of theological jurisprudence was at an end, and the next great name in the history of international law is that of a Dutch lay scholar and diplomat. Hugo Grotius (1583–1645) hardly deserves the soubriquet "father of international law" commonly bestowed on him, for his criteria of "just and unjust wars" are largely derived from the writings of his Catholic predecessors. Perhaps because he was a Protestant invoking the individual conscience rather than churchly authority, and wrote as a jurist (his work is entitled "Concerning the Law of War and Peace"[2]) rather than a churchman, it is to Grotius that most lawyers refer today when describing the foundations of international law.

So far as concerns "just and unjust wars" as a legal concept, however, Grotius is not the beginning but nearly the end of the story. He had a few followers—the Germans Pufendorf and Wolff and the Swiss Emmerich de Vattel—who treated the doctrine seriously, but by the end of the 18th century it was generally disregarded or discredited by governments and writers alike. The principle causes of its decline and virtual disappearance were the Reformation and the growth of nationalism, bringing changes in the structure of European civilization which the concept was ill-equipped to survive.

Until the end of the 16th century, the Pope and other princes of the Church often settled disputes among the temporal rulers, either by their own force or upon request as arbitrators. St. Thomas and his successors were not engaging in mere academic disputation when they pondered the justness of wars, for the Church was deeply and powerfully involved in wars and their consequences. But with the Reformation and the ensuing decline in the Pope's temporal power, the Church's arbitraments were less frequent or significant. The stream of theological jurisprudence soon ran dry, and the 17th century Spaniards had no notable successors.

At the same time the western nation-state, with a nationalist-minded population and nationally organized armed forces, was coming into full flower. Wars played a large part in this process, and a nation's record of victories and defeats began to be regarded as the major theme of its history. In these wars, who was to say on which side justice lay? On such matters the Pope's voice, should he raise it, would no longer be heeded, and since there was no other source of supranational judgment it was left to each nation to make its own decision. The only way that international injustice could be rectified was by war or its threat. Furthermore, with the growth of international trade the concept of neutrality was increasingly important, and the development and observance of "neutral rights" was impossible unless the neutral nations forbore to pass judgment as between the belligerents.

In the course of the 19th century, as Germany and Italy coalesced into nation-states born of wars and new nations sprouted in the wake of the Turkish retreat from Europe, the temper of international law grew increasingly pragmatic. The "just and unjust war" concept was scorned as sentimental rubbish, hopelessly vague in content and impossible to enforce for lack of a tribunal competent to pass judgment. War, in short, was a fact of life that the law must accept.

To be sure, governments would still give reasons for resorting to war that stressed the justice of their cause, and individuals might legitimately entertain beliefs about the morality of a particular war. But none of this was of any *legal* significance. All belligerents started out in identical legal positions and possessed of equal rights. Lieber, progressive and humane as he was with regard to the manners and methods of warfare, had no doubts about its intrinsic validity. "Ever since the foundation of modern nations, and ever since wars have become great national wars," he wrote, "war has come to be acknowledged not to be its own end, but the means to obtain great ends of state . . ." Consequently: "The law of nations allows every sovereign government to make war upon another sovereign state."

And so when in 1914 the lights went out in Europe, although there were lamentations for the death and destruction that loomed and accusations and counter-accusations of blame for bringing on the War, no one said that those responsible (whoever they might be) had committed a crime under international law. After the war had ended, despite the hatreds aroused by four years of carnage, the view still prevailed that launching the war had been a moral outrage but not a crime.[3]

This conclusion was reached and recommended to the Paris Peace Conference by a 15-member "Commission on Responsibilities," charged with investigating the "responsibility of the authors of the war" as well as violations of the laws of war, and proposing appropriate machinery for the trial of those accused. On the matter of responsibility for the war itself, the Commission had no difficulty in finding that the Central Powers (the German and Austro-Hungarian Empires) had "premeditated" the war, acted deliberately "in order to make it unavoidable," and violated the neutrality of Belgium and Luxembourg despite treaty guarantees to which they were parties. These findings certainly met the Augustinian criteria of an "unjust war," and the Commission found the Central Powers guilty of "conduct which the public conscience reproves and history will condemn." But as a legal matter, the Commission declared that "a war of aggression may not be considered as an act directly contrary to positive law, or one which can be successfully brought before a tribunal." Except for confused and bungling efforts to try the ex-Kaiser "for a supreme offence against international morality and the sanctity of treaties,"* the views of the Commission prevailed at the Peace Conference, and the criminal provisions of the Versailles Treaty were confined to violations of the laws of war.

These events sufficiently demonstrate an international consensus in 1919 that to initiate a war—even an aggressive war—was not a crime under international law. But that year may also be taken to mark the beginning of the trend that led to Nuremberg, for the Commission on Responsibilities viewed its own conclusion as revealing a grave shortcoming in the scope of international law, and recommended "that for the future penal sanctions should be provided for such gross outrages." This proposal was not implemented in the Versailles Treaty, and not until the end of the Second World War were any "penal sanctions" authorized. The Commission's recommendation, nonetheless, was the signal of a new international view of the legality of war, the first fruits of which appeared at once in the Covenant of the League of Nations.

The new approach was, unquestionably, the product of the unprecedented scope and destructiveness of the First World War, and especially the greatly increased risks to civilian life stemming from the advent of military air power. The only possible justification for the highly organized slaughter was

---

* This language was part of Article 227 of the Treaty of Versailles, which provided that a "special tribunal" would be established to try "William II of Hohenzollern, formerly German Emperor." The Government of the Netherlands, where the ex-Kaiser had sought refuge, refused to turn him over to the Allies, on the ground that the offense charged was unknown in Dutch law and appeared to be of a political rather than a criminal character.

that it had been a "war to end war," and that aim was the League's chief purpose.

No explicit statement that aggressive war is criminal was made in the Covenant. Its most significant contribution was the establishment of a procedure for international resolution of disputes among its members, and the application of international force against any who, in defiance of the decision, resorted to war. It was a necessary inference from such a determination that the offending *government* was guilty of a crime, though the Covenant left untouched any question of the criminal liability of the individuals, few or many, responsible for their government's unlawful act. Furthermore, the Covenant procedure met what had been the fatal flaw of the "unjust war" concept, by providing for international rather than unilateral determinations of "justness." This precisely fitted the Thomist test, for now there was a higher power to order disputes among nations. That being so, resort to war by individual nations would henceforth be as "unjust" as it had always been for a private person; under the Covenant the only just war would be the use of international force in order to subdue the recalcitrant nation.[*]

The First World War, unlike the Second, was followed by a dozen years of general peace and, toward the end of the twenties, of prosperity and

---

[*] There was, however, a significant gap in the procedure, in that the decision of the superior body (the Council of the League of Nations) had to be unanimous, except for the parties to the dispute themselves. If unanimity was unattainable, then all members were free "to take such action as they shall consider necessary for the maintenance of right and justice." The action might be war, thus legitimized by the League's inaction.

contentment in the western world. On a number of occasions the League peace-keeping machinery was successfully used to forestall or terminate small wars —between Yugoslavia and Albania in 1921, Italy and Greece in 1923, Greece and Bulgaria in 1925, Bolivia and Paraguay in 1928, and Colombia and Peru in 1933. The Locarno and other regional or bilateral nonaggression treaties testified to the pacific temper of western statesmen and peoples.

Outstanding among these between-war efforts to abolish war was the treaty officially entitled "International Treaty for the Renunciation of War as an Instrument of National Policy." On April 6, 1927, the tenth anniversary of the United States' entry into the First World War, the French Foreign Minister, Aristide Briand, suggested that the occasion be celebrated by a Franco-American agreement to outlaw war between the two countries. The Secretary of State, Frank B. Kellogg, proposed that the pact be multilateral, and impetus was given the project by a resolution of the League Assembly unanimously adopted in September, 1927, which described "a war of aggression" as "an international crime" and declared that "all wars of aggression are and shall always be prohibited." The treaty itself —commonly known as the "Pact of Paris" or "Kellogg-Briand Pact," and eventually accepted by the United States, France, and 42 other nations—was signed in August, 1928. Its two substantive articles were:

> *Article 1. The High Contracting Parties solemnly declare . . . that they condemn re-*

69

*course to war for the solution of international controversies, and renounce it as an instrument of national policy in their relations with one another.*

*Article 2. The High Contracting Parties agree that the settlement or solution of all disputes or conflicts, of whatever nature or whatever origin they may be, which may arise among them, shall never be sought except by pacific means.*

The Kellogg-Briand treaty was the highwater mark of the peaceful tide.[4] With the 1930's came economic depression, Adolf Hitler and a surge of militant nationalism in the nations—Germany, Italy and Japan—that later comprised the "Axis powers." The League's peace-keeping procedures were dependent for their effectiveness on the will of its members, especially the major European powers, and the will proved insufficient to check Japan's invasion of China or Italy's conquest of Ethiopia. After 1936 the League's prestige dwindled rapidly, and European crises in Spain, Austria, Czechoslovakia, Lithuania and Albania were resolved, one after another, by unilateral military action on the part of Nazi Germany and Fascist Italy. By 1939, when war came, the League was little more than a relic of better times.

The Second World War raised anew the question pondered by the Commission on Responsibilities and answered in the negative at the end of the First World War. Had the Kellogg-Briand treaty or any other event between the wars sufficiently altered the controlling considerations so that individuals could now be charged with crime under international law on grounds of responsibility for aggressive war?

The problem re-emerged in March, 1944, at meetings of the Legal Committee of the United Nations War Crimes Commission in London.[5] The Czechoslovak member of the Committee, Dr. Bohuslav Ečer, submitted a report on the permissible scope of "retributive action" the thrust of which was that the war was of such terrible and unprecedented dimensions that its initiators should be held criminally responsible. The committee was persuaded, and in May it recommended to the commission that the "war crimes" with which it was concerned should be deemed to include: "The crimes committed for the purpose of preparing or launching the war, irrespective of the territory where these crimes have been committed."

But the commission members were cautious, and doubted that their governments would move so far into unfamiliar legal and political territory. The matter was referred back to the Legal Committee, and in turn to a four-member subcommittee. The American and Dutch members approved the recommendations of the British member, Sir Arnold McNair, and the majority report of the subcommittee concluded that the Kellogg-Briand treaty had not significantly altered the circumstances that had been thought decisive in 1919. Just as in 1919, the majority proposed to recommend that the "outrages" of the Axis leaders be "the subject of formal condemnation," and that penal sanctions should be provided "for the future."

The fourth member of the subcommittee was Dr.

Ećer, who submitted a minority report reiterating his earlier views, and suggesting that the Commission need not take a position on the legality of aggressive war in general, but should declare that the aims and methods of the Axis leaders, and the "total" character of the war they had launched, made them criminally liable.

When the two reports came before the commission in October, 1944, the Australian representative (and future Chairman of the commission), Lord Wright of Durley, was the principal spokesman for the Czech view. As a common law lawyer, Lord Wright was accustomed to find law in developing customs and practices, and for him the Kellogg-Briand pact and other agreements and pronouncements since the First World War were sufficient evidence of a "general consensus of authoritative opinion."*

Opinion in the commission was sharply divided, with the representatives of Britain, France, Greece, the Netherlands and the United States supporting the majority report, and Australia, China, Czechoslovakia, New Zealand, Poland and Yugoslavia on the other side. The division was too even to warrant action either way, and the members decided to consult their respective governments. In the upshot, the commission never came to a decision on the

---

* Lord Wright's views on the nature of international law, it is interesting to note, were in line with those of the Roman Catholic theologians. Suarez had written: "The Precepts of the Law of Nations differ in this from those of civil law, that they are not in writing, but in customs . . . of all or almost all nations . . . if it is introduced by the customs of all nations and binds all, we believe this to be the Law of Nations properly speaking."

issue, and after 1944 it ceased to be the principal forum for its determination.

Between the theologians and Grotians of past centuries, and the diplomats of the between-war years of the present one, there is a difference in the concept of justifiable war that is of great significance today. From St. Augustine to Vattel the test was stated in terms of "just" and "unjust wars," whereas after the First World War the issue was drawn between "aggressive wars" and "defensive wars."

Despite the imprecision and generality of both "just" and "aggressive," there is a substantive and describable difference between the meanings intended by their users. It is true that warfare undertaken to repel and attack was generally regarded by theologians as "just," but this was not necessarily so, and self-defense did not exhaust the entire content of "just," for if one country had a "just" claim or grievance against another, it could "justly" resort to war to enforce its rights. Thus if Prince A had been wronged by Prince B, Prince A's attack would be aggressive yet just, and Prince B's defensive fighting would be unjust, for he should have yielded voluntarily to a righteous claim.

The difficulty with all this, which especially troubled the later scholiasts like Vitoria and Suarez, was that "just" was too open-ended a test, and unilateral determinations of what was "just" were too subjective to constitute anything resembling law. Granted that there is plenty of room for argument about the meaning and application of "aggression," its ambiguities are of narrower range. Furthermore, its specificity was measurably sharpened by the Kellogg-Briand pact's condemnation of war "as an instrument of national policy" or "for the solution of international controversies," for that said pretty plainly that Nation A could *not* use war to enforce a claim, no matter how just, against Nation B. Under the "aggression" test, self-defense is practically the only basis on which it is legitimate to engage in warfare.* On its face at least, this is a much more objective test, more readily satisfied by evidentiary proof, and analogous to legal standards long established in domestic criminal law. And unquestionably it was this circumstance, coupled with the nature of the Hitler wars, that enabled the victorious governments, led by the United States, to take the leap in 1945 that they had shied from in 1918. Presumably according to his own standards, Hitler believed his own wars to be "just." But whatever the historians might ultimately say about the root causes of the Second World War, it was indisputable that neither Poland, Denmark, Norway, Holland, Belgium, Yugoslavia, Greece nor the Soviet Union had attacked Germany. If aggression was the test of criminality, it seemed clear where the blame lay.

The reason that the United Nations War Crimes Commission was crowded off the stage, and that the

---

* This appears now to approximate the position of the Roman Catholic Church as stated in the "Pastoral Constitution on the Church in the Modern World, Dec. 7, 1965," adopted at the Second Vatican Council:⁶ "As long as the danger of war remains and there is no competent and sufficiently powerful authority at the international level, governments cannot be denied the right to legitimate defense once every means of peaceful settlement has been exhausted."

Nuremberg trials took place, was that legally trained men in the seats of power in Washington concluded that German aggression could be judicially proved, that the future peace of the world would be promoted by an international determination that aggressive warfare is a crime under international law, and that those responsible may be punished. Chief among the architects of Nuremberg was Henry L. Stimson, who had been Secretary of War under President William Howard Taft, Secretary of State under Herbert Hoover, and was again Secretary of War under Franklin D. Roosevelt; others closely involved included Attorney General Francis Biddle, Judge Samuel Rosenman of the White House staff and, after Roosevelt's death, Justice Robert H. Jackson, who took leave from the Supreme Court of the United States to take charge of American interests in the war crimes field and serve as chief prosecutor.

The purpose of charging the Axis leaders with criminal responsibility for launching wars of aggression, and trying them before an internationally constituted tribunal, was part of the "Nuremberg project"* from its inception in the late fall of 1944. It was a design more readily accomplished by a high-level political decision than by committees of international lawyers for, as has been seen, in professional circles there still was sharp disagreement. The laws of war had been considered, compiled and codified in The Hague and Geneva conventions,

---

* At the outset, of course, it was not known where the trials would be held. It was not until August, 1945, that Nuremberg was definitely selected as the site.

and enforced by courts-martial and military commissions for many years past; there was no substantial disagreement about their judicial enforceability. But the crime of engaging in aggressive warfare—the "crime against peace" as it was called at Nuremberg—had never before been the basis of a charge or proceeding of any description.

Unprecedented as it was, the inclusion of the aggressive war charge was bound to enmesh the Nuremberg proceedings in lasting controversy, although in the upshot no man suffered death and few any lesser penalty on that basis. Opinions still differ on whether Stimson, Jackson and their colleagues were well-advised to press the proposition as they did. We need not wrestle here with might-have-beens. Indisputably it was a cardinal part of the postwar policy of the United States Government to establish the criminality under international law of aggressive warfare, and the Nuremberg and Tokyo trials were the vehicles by which that purpose was accomplished. And if one seeks the reasons for that policy, they are nowhere better stated than in Jackson's progress report to President Truman in June, 1945, a few months before the trials began:

> . . . In untroubled times, progress toward an effective rule of law in the international community is slow indeed. Inertia rests more heavily upon the society of nations than upon any other society. Now we stand at one of those rare moments when the thought and institutions and habits of the world have been shaken by the impact of world war on the lives of count-

*less millions. Such occasions rarely come and quickly pass. We are put under a heavy responsibility to see that our behavior during this unsettled period will direct the world's thought toward a firmer enforcement of the laws of international conduct, so as to make war less attractive to those who have governments and the destinies of peoples in their power.*

# 4 / Nuremberg

THE UNITED NATIONS and the Nuremberg trials were virtually twin offspring of the Allied negotiations and agreements with respect to the peace that would follow victory. It was at the Moscow Conference in October, 1943, that Churchill, Roosevelt and Stalin issued joint declarations pledging their countries to the establishment of an international organization to maintain peace and security, and to the post-war trial and punishment of German war criminals. It was at the San Francisco Conference in the spring of 1945 that the United Nations was organized, and that the first discussions looking to the establishment of an international war crimes tribunal were conducted among the four principal Allies—Britain, France, the Soviet Union and the United States. The Charter of the

United Nations was signed at San Francisco on June 26, 1945, and the Agreement embodying the Charter of the International Military Tribunal was signed on Aug. 8, 1945, at London.

Different as the twins were, they shared the same two basic purposes: promoting peaceful rather than warlike settlement of international disputes, and humanitarian governmental policies. Thus the Charter of the United Nations declared the organization's purposes to be "the prevention and removal of threats to the peace . . . and the suppression of acts of aggression or other breaches of the peace," while the London Charter specified as "crimes against peace" the "planning, preparation, initiation, or waging of a war of aggression, or a war in violation of international treaties, agreements or assurances." The United Nations was dedicated to "encouraging respect for human rights and for fundamental freedoms for all without distinction as to race, sex, language, or religion," and the London Charter condemned not only "war crimes" but also "crimes against humanity," including "persecutions on political, racial, or religious grounds." Essentially, the Nuremberg trials were intended to bring the weight of law and criminal sanctions to bear in support of the peaceful and humanitarian principles that the United Nations was to promote by consultation and collective action.

The subsequent history of the United Nations has shown a disturbing similarity to that of the League of Nations, insofar as an early period of substantial contribution to the peace of the world has given way to one of declining influence. One need only mention Greece, the Berlin airlift confrontation, and the soon-ended Kashmiri war between India and Pakistan, to appreciate the value of the United Nations' past services to the cause of peace. But the Cuban crisis was settled directly between Washington and Moscow, and in recent years the major international issues have appeared to lie beyond the United Nations' effective reach. This has been notably true of the Vietnam war, and is a factor of considerable importance in assessing America's responsibility for its continuation and intensification.

The Nuremberg trials, of course, were not conceived as a continuing enterprise, but as an episode that would leave an enduring juridical monument, to mark a giant step in the growth of international law. In the preceding chapters we have traced the course of events and the developing doctrines that led to Nuremberg, Tokyo and the other major war crimes trials of the Second World War. What did Nuremberg add to what was there before?

In terms of international law, the most important single feature of the Nuremberg trials was that the tribunals were established by international authority, and exercised a jurisdiction internationally conferred. Previously, as we have seen, the laws of war had been enforced by military courts established by the armed forces of the aggrieved nation and, while those laws were international, the power to enforce them was given by their own government alone. But the International Military Tribunal that conducted the first Nuremberg trial was established under the four-power London Charter, to which[23] other nations adhered; the ensuing Nuremberg trials were held under a comparable authorization* from the same four powers that signed the London Charter; the Tokyo trial was conducted by the 11-member International Military Tribunal for the Far East, under the authority of the 10-nation Far Eastern Commission.[1]

The international constitution of these war crimes tribunals was almost but not wholly unprecedented. Scholarship has disclosed[2] an interesting forerunner of Nuremberg in the trial of Peter von Hagenbach at the German city of Breisach in 1474. The accused had served Duke Charles ("the Bold") of Burgundy as Governor of Breisach and adjacent territory on the Upper Rhine, and had inaugurated a reign of terror for which, after Charles's defeat and death, Hagenbach was charged with conduct that "trampled under foot the laws of God and man" and constituted crimes under natural law. The prosecutor was Henry Iselin of Basle, and since Swiss merchants traveling to and from the Frankfurt Fair had been among his victims, Hagenbach was tried before a bench that included Swiss as well as Alsatian and German judges. In language amazingly anticipatory of Henry Wirz's plea to the Andersonville court four centuries later, the defendant invoked the doctrine of superior orders: "Is it not known that soldiers owe absolute obedience to their superiors? Had not the Duke by his presence sub-

---

* Control Council Law No. 10, promulgated on Dec. 20, 1945, by the representatives of the four powers (Britain, France, the Soviet Union, and the United States) occupying Germany and embodying provisions comparable but not identical to those of the London Charter.

sequently confirmed and ratified all that had been done in his name?" The judges, however, were unimpressed, and Hagenbach was convicted and beheaded in the marketplace of Breisach.

The episode shows that the roots of international penal law run deep, but there appear to be no other notable precedents for its enforcement by an international tribunal.* The significance of the international character of the Nuremberg and Tokyo tribunals was a recognition of the inadequacy of single-nation courts for authoritative interpretations of international law, and the necessity of establishing international jurisdiction and working out acceptable international procedures if international penal law was to develop at all satisfactorily. The shortcoming of the tribunals was that, although international, they were unilateral; they were constituted by the victor nations and had jurisdiction only over the vanquished, and this circumstance has remained a negative factor in subsequent evaluation of the trials.

A second remarkable feature of the trials was that they brought about a great expansion of the principle that individuals may be held criminally liable under international law, even though their conduct was valid under, or even required by, domestic law. Intrinsically, this was not a new concept, for the laws of war had always been regarded as binding on both governments and individuals, and beyond the reach of abrogation by local law. Henry Wirz's

---

* Neither the Permanent Court of International Justice established in 1920, nor its successor the International Court of Justice which is the judicial organ of the United Nations, was given any criminal jurisdiction over individuals.

defense would have been no more successful had he been able to show that atrocious treatment of Union prisoners was required by a Confederate statute as well as by General Winder's order.

But prior to Nuremberg the individuals against whom the laws of war had been enforced were, for the most part, ordinary soldiers or officers of middling or low rank. At Nuremberg and Tokyo, on the other hand, nearly all the defendants stood at or near the top of the military or civilian hierarchy. Their punishment gave real meaning to the injunction, long written in the military codes and manuals, that the primary responsibility for war crimes committed pursuant to order rests on those in authority who gave the orders.

The Nuremberg extensions of criminal liability were not only vertical but also horizontal. Generals and admirals were by no means the only defendants. Cabinet ministers and other civilian officials were a majority of those put to trial, and there were also a number of individuals who were "private" in the sense that their criminal liability was not primarily charged on the basis of whatever government connections they may have had, but by reason of their responsibilities as directors of large industrial concerns where foreign "slave" labor was extensively utilized under inhumane conditions.

This expansion of individual liability did not, of course, embrace the supposed "Nuremberg principle" quoted in the introduction that "a citizen must not go along with policies he believes to be wrong."[3] But it did reaffirm and enforce in new spheres the principle that the laws of war, and some other rules of international law, are superior to domestic law, and that individuals may be held accountable to them. As the International Tribunal at Nuremberg put the matter in its judgment:

> . . . *individuals have international duties which transcend the national obligations of obedience imposed by the individual state. He who violates the laws of war cannot obtain immunity while acting in pursuance of the authority of the state if the state in authorizing action moves outside its competence under international law.*[4]

In terms of substantive international law, and in the mind of the general public, the salient feature of the Nuremberg trials was the decision that individuals could be held guilty for participation in the planning and waging of "a war of aggression."

Strictly speaking, the establishing of aggressive war as an international crime was accomplished not by the Tribunal but by the London Charter, which specified "crimes against peace" as one of the three types of crimes that might be charged. The Tribunal in its judgment acknowledged the Charter as "binding upon the Tribunal," and deduced that "it is therefore not strictly necessary to consider whether and to what extent aggressive war was a crime before the execution of the London Agreement." Not content to rest on the Charter alone, however, the Tribunal included a long passage in support of the conclusion that the Kellogg-Briand and other recent treaties and international resolutions had made aggressive war "not merely illegal, but criminal." The Tokyo and later Nuremberg tribunals reached the same result.*

Having thus confirmed the legitimacy of the charge, the Nuremberg courts had little difficulty in deciding that Germany's wars against Poland, Denmark, Norway, Belgium, the Netherlands, Luxembourg, Yugoslavia, Greece, the Soviet Union and the United States were aggressive wars. The Tokyo tribunal came to the same conclusion with respect to Japan's wars against China, the British Commonwealth, France, the Netherlands, the Soviet Union and the United States. At Nuremberg the courts' task was greatly aided by the circumstances that voluminous German military and diplomatic records had fallen into Allied hands at the end of the war, that Germans are meticulous record-makers and that Hitler and some of his subordinates had revealed their aggressive intentions very explicitly in the documents that thus became available as evidence at the trials.

There remained, however, the far more difficult question of which, if any, of the individual defendants could be held guilty of the "crime against peace." By what standards should this sort of criminal liability be determined? It takes a number to plan and many to wage war, but knowledge of its aggressive or defensive character may be confined to a small group, and even among the members of the inner circle there may be disagreement. In Nazi Germany those close to Hitler and present at the

* The Tokyo court, however, was not unanimous on this point; the Indian judge, R. M. Pal, dissented, and the Dutch judge, Bernard V. A. Roling, concurred on what were tantamount to political rather than juridical grounds.

meetings where he revealed his plans might legitimately be held to share his guilt, and at the first Nuremberg trial most of the 12 (out of 22) defendants convicted on the aggressive war charges were of that description.

But one of them, Karl Doenitz, was only a commodore and commander of the small U-boat arm when the war began; the Tribunal found that he had neither been present at Hitler's conferences nor informed about his plans, and based the conviction on the fact that Doenitz "waged" aggressive war because his submarines "were fully prepared to wage war." On that basis every commander of combat troops or ships would have been equally guilty, but the Tribunal's opinion showed no awareness of these far-reaching implications. Inferentially though not explicitly the judgment on Doenitz was repudiated by a later Nuremberg court that acquitted on the same charge commanders of much higher rank than Doenitz on the ground that they were not at the "policy level."[5]

Except for Doenitz, the first Nuremberg tribunal took a restricted view of the scope of individual liability on the aggressive war charge. The later Nuremberg tribunals were even more conservative in this respect, acquitting 49 of the 52 defendants so charged, including all of the military leaders and industrialists. One of the tribunals did, however, convict three high-ranking civilian officials, and also ruled that Germany's destruction of Austrian and Czechoslovak independence in 1938 and 1939 had been military invasions and therefore aggressive wars, although there had been no resistance.

The Tokyo tribunal was confronted with quite a different problem of responsibility, since there was no Japanese leader who at all corresponded to Hitler, and government policies were the product of pressures and counterpressures of powerful military (17 of the defendants were military men) and political cliques. Furthermore, the relevant time period was much longer for Japan than for Germany, as the aggressive war against China was determined to have begun in Manchuria in 1931. On the whole the Tokyo judges were readier than those at Nuremberg to find criminal liability in this accusation. They convicted all but one of the 25 defendants on the charge, in every case on the basis that the accused had participated in the formulation of Japan's aggressive policies.

In all, accordingly, 15 Germans and 24 Japanese were convicted of planning or waging aggressive war.* Of the Japanese, 15 were convicted on no other charge, and all but one (who was given a 20-year term) were sentenced to life imprisonment. Of the 15 Germans, all but one were also found guilty of violations of the laws of war; the single exception was the half-mad Rudolf Hess, who was given

---

* Another German (Artur Greiser, the Nazi leader in Danzig) was convicted in July, 1946 by the Supreme National Tribunal of Poland of various crimes including waging aggressive war, and to him goes the dubious honor of being the first person ever convicted on such a charge. Another Japanese, General Takeshi Sakai, was convicted in August, 1946, on comparable charges, in connection with Japan's aggressive war against China, by a Chinese war crimes tribunal in Nanking. Both Greiser and Sakai were condemned to death.

Probably because of Italy's capitulation in 1943 and the lynching of Benito Mussolini at the end of the war, no Italian was accused of crimes against peace. In fact, there were no noteworthy war crimes trials of Italians, despite the fact that the jurisdiction of the International Military Tribunal covered "the European Axis countries."

a life sentence and, by a cruel irony, is the only Nuremberg defendant still in custody. Thus none of the 16 persons convicted only on aggressive war charges received the death penalty, a restraint on the part of the courts that no doubt reflected the unprecedented nature of the charge.

At Nuremberg there were 59 acquittals on the aggressive war charge, so that the ratio of acquittals to convictions was nearly four to one. This result is another demonstration of the narrow range of liability that the tribunals found appropriate to the nature of the offense. On ordinary principles of criminal liability, conviction would follow if it were proved that a war was in fact aggressive, that the accused believed it to be aggressive, and nonetheless participated in waging it. Except in the case of Doenitz, however, the tribunals applied more stringent standards. In the cases against the directors of the Krupp and I. G. Farben industries, the test of knowledge was strictly applied; even if the defendants had reason to believe that aggressive wars were in contemplation, they were not guilty because they were not privy to Hitler's personal plans and aims. In the case against high-ranking military leaders, even such privity did not suffice, because the accused did not have "actual power to shape and influence the policy of their nation, prepare for, or lead their country into or in an aggressive war."[6]

If, on the assumption that American operations in Vietnam constitute waging aggressive war, questions were to be raised today concerning the criminal liability of individual Americans under the Nuremberg and Tokyo principles, the answer would have to be found within the limits that are marked by these decisions.

For reasons that have already been suggested,[7] the Nuremberg and Tokyo trials shed little new light on the laws of war relating to the use of weapons. The charges based on submarine warfare were totally discounted at Nuremberg, and no such accusations were made in Tokyo. Aerial bombardment had been used so extensively and ruthlessly on the Allied as well as the Axis side that neither at Nuremberg nor Tokyo was the issue made a part of the trials.

It was, accordingly, the laws of war with respect to prisoners and the treatment of civilians by military occupation forces that were primarily involved in these cases. On the whole there was no serious question about the criminality of the conduct charged or difficulty in proving that it had in fact occurred, and the only issues were whether those accused were responsible and, if so, whether or not there were mitigating circumstances.

The conduct disclosed at Nuremberg did not disclose new types of crime; murder, maiming, enslavement, ravage, and plunder are a familiar litany. What was unique about the Nazi conquests, especially in eastern Europe, was the enormous scope of the atrocities, and the systematic planning and meticulous execution of these hideous enterprises. In 1941, for example, the German Army invaded Russia under orders from the high command that stripped the military courts of jurisdiction over offenses committed by enemy civilians, who were remitted to summary treatment by troop commanders on the spot, and that directed that German soldiers were not to be prosecuted for offenses against Russian civilians unless it was necessary for the discipline or security of the German forces.[8] Numerous other orders issued at the highest level instructed the troops that "considerations of international law are out of place" in dealing with Bolshevists, ordered the execution of commandos even if captured in uniform and in conditions of safety, encouraged the execution of "50 to 100" hostages for every German soldier killed by partisans and established special police units to accompany the army and kill all the Jews discovered in the occupied areas.

The picture that emerged in the Tokyo and other trials in the Far East was significantly different in that there were no comparable general orders. The Japanese did not, as did the Germans, carefully organize a program of atrocities. Their conduct during the war appears to have been much more spontaneous, and governed by the life-style of the field commanders on the spot. Of the 25 Tokyo defendants, only five were found guilty of ordering or otherwise approving violations of the laws of war, and in only two of these cases (both relating to the unlawful employment of prisoners of war in Burma) do the crimes appear to have been ordered by the Japanese Government. The three other defendants convicted of war crimes were found guilty only on the basis that they did not fulfill their duty to insure lawful conduct on the part of subordinates.

The imposition of liability for the criminal acts of others was carried a long way in several cases, of

which perhaps the most striking is that of Koki
Hirota, who served briefly as Prime Minister and
for several years as Foreign Minister between 1933
and May, 1938, after which he held no office
whatever. The so-called "rape of Nanking" by Japanese forces occurred during the winter of 1937–38,
when Hirota was Foreign Minister. Upon receiving
early reports of the atrocities, he demanded and
received assurances from the War Ministry that
they would be stopped. But they continued, and the
Tokyo tribunal found Hirota guilty because he "was
derelict in his duty in not insisting before the Cabinet that immediate action be taken to put an end to
the atrocities," and "was content to rely on assurances which he knew were not being implemented."
On this basis, coupled with his conviction on the
aggressive war charge, Hirota was sentenced to be
hanged.

The most noteworthy case of capital punishment
for a commander's failure to discharge his responsibilities was not tried before the Nuremberg or
Tokyo tribunals, but by a United States military
commission in Manila. The defendant was General
Tomayuki Yamashita, the Japanese Army commander in the Philippine Islands during the closing
months of the war. During that time, as the undisputed evidence showed, the conduct of the Japanese
occupation forces degenerated rapidly, and there
were numerous massacres of prisoners of war and
slaughter of civilians, as well as burning and loot-
ing. There was no charge that General Yamashita
had approved, much less ordered these barbarities,
and no evidence that he knew of them other than

the inference that he must have because of their extent. The defense showed that by the time he took command the Japanese military position in Luzon was precarious because of the American victory at Leyte, the tightening naval blockade and heavy allied bombardments, so that Yamashita's communications and control of his forces rapidly disintegrated. Nevertheless, the tribunal found Yamashita guilty on the ground that he had "failed to provide effective control of his troops as required by the circumstances," and sentenced him to death by hanging. The sentence was confirmed by General MacArthur, and the validity of the proceedings was sustained by the United States Supreme Court.[9]

To summarize, the Nuremberg, Tokyo and other post-World War II war crimes trials brought to the development of the international penal law of war an international jurisdiction, a strong affirmation of the individual's obligation to comply with internationally recognized standards of conduct, a first enforcement within narrow limits of the concept of "crimes against peace," and a considerable expansion of the area of criminal liability for violations of the laws of war.

Outside the legal dimension, however, the Nuremberg trials had perhaps an even more significant impact on the governments and peoples of the world, in spreading a sense of the moral and political importance of the issues with which the trials were concerned. Before Nuremberg, the laws of war were embodied in professional military tradition, field manuals, international law treatises and occasionally in little-noticed court-martial proceedings. Nuremberg made them the preoccupation of great statesmen and generals, and the stuff of newspaper headlines.

The setting at Nuremberg was prestigious and highly dramatic. The defendants were colorful and infamous or notorious, and the spectacle of their confrontation with the documents, films, and other records of their doings was now disgusting, now poignant, and always gripping. Lawyers of great renown appeared at the bar of the courts, and Robert Jackson's extraordinary gift for the written word projected the terrible events and searching issues in unforgettable language.

Military courts and commissions have customarily rendered their judgments stark and unsupported by opinions giving the reasons for their decisions. The Nuremberg and Tokyo judgments, in contrast, were all based on extensive opinions detailing the evidence and analyzing the factual and legal issues, in the fashion of appellate tribunals generally. Needless to say they were not of uniform quality, and often reflected the logical shortcomings of compromise, the marks of which commonly mar the opinions of multi-member tribunals. But the process was *professional* in a way seldom achieved in military courts, and the records and judgments in these trials provided a much-needed foundation for a corpus of judge-made international penal law. The results of the trials commended themselves to the newly formed United Nations, and on Dec. 11, 1946, the General Assembly adopted a resolution affirming "the principles of international law recognized by the Charter of the Nuremberg Tribunal and the judgment of the Tribunal."

However history may ultimately assess the wisdom or unwisdom of the war crimes trials, one thing is indisputable: At their conclusion, the United States Government stood legally, politically and morally committed to the principles enunciated in the charters and judgments of the tribunals. The President of the United States, on the recommendation of the Departments of State, War and Justice, approved the war crimes programs. Thirty or more American judges, drawn from the appellate benches of the states from Massachusetts to Oregon, and Minnesota to Georgia, conducted the later Nuremberg trials and wrote the opinions. General Douglas MacArthur, under authority of the Far Eastern Commission, established the Tokyo tribunal and confirmed the sentences it imposed, and it was under his authority as the highest American military officer in the Far East that the Yamashita and other such proceedings were held. The United States delegation to the United Nations presented the resolution by which the General Assembly endorsed the Nuremberg principles.

Thus the integrity of the nation is staked on those principles, and today the question is how they apply to our conduct of the war in Vietnam, and whether the United States Government is prepared to face the consequences of their application.

# 5 / Aggressive War, Vietnam and the Courts

"At the time of the Nuremberg trials," wrote the late Thurman Arnold, eminent writer, judge and staunch defender of President Johnson's Vietnam policies, "those who write the think columns in our press, such as Walter Lippmann, and independent organizations of intellectuals . . . and liberal professors on our campuses, acclaimed the principle of the outlawing of aggressive war as a great step forward in international law. Today they are bending every effort to prevent the enforcement of the principle that Nuremberg announced to the world. . . . They are encouraging Hanoi to believe that if it will only hang on the United States will abandon its attempt to enforce the Nuremberg principle in Asia." Official voices take up the same theme. "The indelible lesson . . . is that the time to stop aggression is at its very beginning," Secretary of State Dean Rusk told the American Society of International Law. "Surely we have learned over the past three decades that the acceptance of aggression leads only to a sure catastrophe. Surely we have learned that the aggressor must face the consequences of his action . . ."[1]

On what does this pro-United States invocation of Nuremberg and its principles rest? Essentially, it is a three-step proposition: (1) that North Vietnam attacked South Vietnam in violation of Article 2 of the United Nations Charter, (2) that South Vietnam was entitled to use force to repel the unlawful attack, and (3) that the United States is justified in joining South Vietnam in "collective defense" under Article 51 of the Charter.

But among those opposed to our policy in Vietnam, Nuremberg is cited even more frequently. "It may appear ironic," declares the National Lawyers Guild, "that the first serious effort to revitalize Nuremberg into a binding legal and moral precedent has been undertaken by citizens of this country who assert that their own government has engaged in an illegal war in Vietnam in violation of international law and morality." And again, in the words of Eric Norden: "Our actions in Vietnam fall within the prohibited classifications of warfare set down at Nuremberg . . . the United States is clearly guilty of 'War Crimes,' 'Crimes against Peace' and 'Crimes against Humanity,' crimes for which the top German leaders were either imprisoned or executed."[2]

So far as it concerns aggressive warfare, the case

for these stark accusations is based on the conclusions that both South Vietnam and the United States violated the Geneva Declaration of 1954 by hostile acts against the North, unlawful rearmament, and refusal to carry out the 1956 national elections provided for in the Declaration, and that the United States likewise violated the United Nations Charter by bombing North Vietnam.

Eminently respectable and learned voices are raised on both sides of the debate. By what standards may it be judged? Critics of the Nuremberg condemnation of "aggressive war" often complain that neither the London Charter nor the tribunals' opinions embodied a definition of the concept. Is definition feasible, and would it help in identifying the aggressor in Vietnam? At the conferences during which the London Charter was formulated, the United States proffered two proposed definitions. But neither was accepted, and the Russian delegate, in words reminiscent of the man who doesn't know much about music but knows what he likes, declared: "When people speak about aggression, they know what that means, but, when they come to define it, they come up against difficulties which as yet it has not been possible to overcome."[3] And in 1950, the Reporter to the International Law Commission of the United Nations concluded, even more bluntly, that any attempt to define aggression "would prove to be a pure waste of time."[4]

That may be an overstatement, but certainly efforts at a definite formulation have not yet been successful. However, this is very commonly the case with general concepts, many of which are indispensable tools of law and philosophy. The Constitution of the United States contains numerous crucial phrases that equally defy definition: "Due process of law" and "unreasonable searches and seizures" come readily to mind. They are also to be found in common criminal and civil law—for example "negligence" or "reasonable doubt." The meaning of such words and phrases can be illuminated by descriptive comments, but invariably these also employ expressions of imprecise or imponderable content.

The lack of a satisfactory definition of "aggressive war" therefore, should not be taken as a sufficient argument against its use as a description of unlawful international conduct. In fact, as the discussion and application of the standard since it came into common parlance reveals, it is not significantly different from the tests for the lawful use of defensive force in our domestic criminal law. As we have already seen, the parallelism is of long standing. There is remarkable similarity between the criteria stated by Suarez and Grotius for distinguishing the just from the unjust war, and the provision of the New York Penal Law specifying the circumstances under which force may rightfully be used: to defend one's self, one's property or to assist other persons engaged in defending themselves or their property. [5]

Over the course of time, the law has developed reasonably satisfactory statutory and judicial formulations of this right of self-defense. But there are no self-operating definitions. The policeman who comes upon a fracas may find it difficult or impossible to decide whether Cohen or Kelly struck the first blow, and the doubts may be equally impossible to dispel when the matter comes into court. And if run-of-the-mill criminal cases commonly present such difficulties, it is hardly surprising to encounter them in international conflicts. The question of initial responsibility, which is the essence of "aggression," may be vexingly complicated, as the Arab-Israeli hostilities abundantly demonstrate. And while there are many on both sides of the Vietnam dispute who declare that the original blamelessness or blameworthiness of the United States is readily demonstrable, the depth of disagreement among men of integrity and intelligence suggests that at least the issues are far from simple.

In practical terms, what difference does it make whether the American involvement in Vietnam is legal or illegal under the Nuremberg principles? Today there is no longer an international tribunal competent to render judgment. But the issue is being dramatically projected in a variety of domestic circumstances. May a soldier under orders to proceed to Vietnam refuse on the ground that he should not participate in an illegal war? May a draft registrant refuse induction on that basis? May taxpayers similarly persuaded of the war's illegality withhold a symbolic or proportionate part of their payments?

These and comparable questions, calling for a determination of the legality of our Government's action in Vietnam, are being pressed before our domestic courts in a host of cases. Should the courts undertake to make such a determination? A strong affirmative opinion has been voiced by Richard A. Falk, Professor of International Law at Princeton:

> . . . the reassertion of an active judicial role in this area would appear to be a creative contribution to the doctrine of separation of powers in the war-peace context. . . . In addition, those who seek access to the courts in order to test the legality of the war—for instance, by refusing to pay all or part of their income taxes—are entitled to a substantive determination of the issue . . . it is important that judges become persuaded of their competence and responsibility to restrain the execution of government policy by either executive or legislative institutions if such policy is found to exceed the boundaries set by international law.[6]

Thus far the Supreme Court has not heeded Professor Falk's call to battle, but the issue rings loudly in the lower court reports and law reviews. *Should* the Supreme Court engage itself with this issue? And if so, what would be the principles and problems attending such an adjudication?

We may best begin by taking a brief look at the merits of the aggression issue, not in order to answer it, but for an understanding of the range and complexity of its components. An answer would involve the interpretation of numerous treaties and other international documents, including the United Nations Charter, the Geneva Declaration of July 21, 1954, the reports of the International Control Commission established under the Geneva agreement, and the Southeast Asia Collective Defense Treaty (SEATO). It would involve the examination of hotly controverted evidentiary questions, such as when the infiltration of North Vietnamese guerrillas into South Vietnam began, and whether American destroyers were in fact attacked, or reasonably believed to have been attacked, by North Vietnamese torpedo boats in the Tonkin Gulf in the summer of 1964. It would involve scrutiny of the information available to, and the intentions of, the President of the United States and the military and civilian officials who helped him to shape and execute our policies and operations in Vietnam.

One example may serve to demonstrate the complexity of these issues. At Geneva in 1954 the dividing line between North and South Vietnam was drawn at the 17th Parallel. Indisputably, the ground fighting has all taken place in South Vietnam; it is the North Vietnamese who have joined the Vietcong "south of the border" and are seeking to subvert the Government of South Vietnam. On its face this would seem strong evidence that it is the North Vietnamese who are using war "as an instrument of national policy" (to echo the Kellogg-Briand pact language) and are the aggressors. Indeed Professor John Norton Moore, one of the stoutest academic supporters of American policy, makes much of this very point: "As both Korea and Vietnam demonstrate, one of the greatest threats to world order today is external intervention seeking coercive change across a boundary separating the *de facto* halves of a cold-war divided country. This is a major reason why it is crucial that international legal scholars clearly condemn the strategy of Hanoi in seeking coercive change across such a cold-war dividing line."[7]

But the matter is not at all that simple. The Geneva agreement of 1954 did not purport to establish two nations, but two "zones," and explicitly declared that "the military demarcation line is provisional and should not in any way be interpreted as constituting a political or territorial boundary." It was the basis for a cease-fire, and the purpose of the zones was specified as "regrouping." The agreement further provided for "free" nationwide elections, to be held in 1956, as the basis for a government based on "the principles of independence, unity and territorial integrity." But South Vietnam, with the support of the United States (which had not signed the Geneva agreement), declined to proceed with the elections on the ground that conditions in North Vietnam were not "free"; consequently the two zones took on the attributes of independent states, with South Vietnam in alliance with the United States. Many international lawyers support the North Vietnamese contention that the Geneva agreements were violated by the refusal to hold elections and unify the country, and that the demarcation line is not properly to be regarded as an international boundary. Consequently, it is said, the North Vietnamese were justified in aiding the Vietcong in South Vietnam, who are seeking to establish a government favorable to unification in line with the purpose of the Geneva agreement.

An American court undertaking to pass judgment on the legality of our Vietnam actions would have to review these and numerous other questions of comparable difficulty and complexity with little guidance from the Nuremberg and Tokyo judgments. Whatever might be said about the long-range causes of the Second World War, there was little question about who attacked whom, and the issue of aggression was comparatively easy to adjudicate.

There are also the vexed questions of intent and motive. At Nuremberg and Tokyo individuals were on trial, and it was possible to declare the wars to be aggressive because of their proven intentions and declarations. But if the issue arises not in a trial of persons accused of crimes against peace, but as a defense in a draft or tax case, it is the "government's" intentions that are called in question. The "government" is not an individual and cannot be said to have intentions of its own, and it might well transpire that the intentions and motives of government leaders were very diverse. Some might in good faith believe, in line with the arguments of Dean Rusk and Thurman Arnold, that the United Nations Charter and the SEATO treaty justified or even required intervention to protect South Vietnam from aggression. Others might talk this language only to conceal the intention to exploit South Vietnam as an American military base to "contain" Communism, or to dominate Southeast Asia and its enormous natural resources. In terms of individual guilt of crimes against peace, the question of intent might be decisive. But where only the "government" is the focus of inquiry, it might be quite impossible to determine the intent with which a particular decision was taken.

In this connection, it may be remarked that the policy-making machinery of the United States resembles much more that of the Japanese as it emerged at the Tokyo trial, than that of Nazi Germany. *"L'Etat, c'est moi,"* said Louis XIV, and Adolf Hitler could truthfully have echoed his words. Hitler's intention *was* the intention of the German Government. But there was no comparable figure in Tokyo, nor has there been in Washington. The President is a focus, but around him there are diverse and shifting groups and combinations of powerful military and civilian leaders, and the Congress likewise has its part to play. Declarations of intent in official documents are designed to be exculpatory, and are often less than candid, to say the least.

In summary, the nature of the issues that would have to be explored in assessing the legality, under the Nuremberg principles, of American participation in the Vietnamese war would present enormous difficulties to any court, and especially to a domestic court of one of the belligerents, convened during the course of hostilities. This is not a conclusive argument against making the attempt, but it is certainly a factor to be weighed in deciding whether or not this is a fit subject for judicial decision.

There is another question concerning the legality of our Vietnam involvement that is not a matter of Nuremberg or other international law principles, but is closely interlocked with them, both legally and politically. This other issue involves the respective powers of the Congress and the President in the fields of foreign relations and war-making. The tension between the two arises from the constitutional provisions that give Congress the power "to declare War," to "raise and support Armies" and "provide and maintain a Navy," and to "make Rules for the Government and Regulation of the land and naval Forces," while specifying also that the President "shall be Commander-in-Chief of the Army and Navy of the United States." Essentially, the contention is that the President has no authority to commit the armed forces to battle in Vietnam without Congressional authority, that no such authority has been given, and that the courts should, if properly called upon, declare the President's actions in Vietnam unconstitutional and subject to judicial restraint.

The constitutional provisions were originally intended to give Congress the principal power of decision as between war and peace. Chief Justice John Marshall, indeed, went so far as to say that "the whole powers of war" were "vested in Congress."[8] The Founding Fathers, however, were well aware that the President must have authority to "repel sudden attacks," as Oliver Ellsworth put it, and the course of events soon led to a very broad interpretation of that phrase. During the Barbary Wars President Jefferson took a very cautious view of his powers, which was hotly disputed by Alexander Hamilton. The latter conceded that it was "the peculiar province of Congress, *when the nation is at peace,* to change that state into a state of war . . . in other words, it belongs to Congress only *to go to War*." However, "when a foreign nation declares, or openly and avowedly makes war upon the United States, they are then by the very fact *already at war,* and any declaration on the part of Congress is nugatory; it is at least unnecessary."

Translated into modern terminology, Hamilton's distinction is drawn between "aggressive" and "defensive" wars. He wrote at a time when Grotian notions had gone out of fashion, and war was, in Lieber's phrase, "the means to obtain great ends of state." But the consequence of Hamilton's view under the United Nations Charter and the Nuremberg principles is indeed curious. If no Congressional authority is needed for defensive wars, and if aggressive wars are outlawed, then there is no room left for necessary and valid Congressional declarations of war, except perhaps in going to the aid of another country that has been wrongfully attacked.

In any event, Hamilton's expansionist approach to Presidential war powers prevailed, and today is conceived far more broadly than even he would have thought possible. In a military sense the world has diminished in size, and old distinctions between "direct attack" and "indirect threat" are blurred. Since the Second World War, all five Presidents— Truman in Korea, Eisenhower in Lebanon, Kennedy in Cuba, Johnson in Vietnam and the Dominican Republic, and Nixon in Cambodia—have taken military action in foreign parts on the basis of their authority as Commander-in-Chief, without Congressional sanction. A 1966 State Department public statement on "The Legality of United States Participation in the Defense of Viet-Nam" declares that the President, as Commander-in-Chief, has "the power to deploy American forces abroad and commit them to military operations when the President deems such action necessary to maintain the security and defense of the United States."[9]

That, of course, is a 180-degree swing from John Marshall's view of the matter, and a virtual erasure of the Congressional role. The tortured course of the Vietnam war both at home and abroad, capped by President Nixon's Cambodian adventure, has aroused strong feeling in Congress that the executive power has been pushed much too far. During the Korean war President Truman, to avert a strike, seized the nation's steel mills and justified the act under his constitutional powers, without Congressional authority. The Supreme Court spanked him sharply, ruling that the President's powers as Commander-in-Chief did not support the seizure.[10] There has never been a comparable judicial test of the President's power to commit troops to foreign wars, but if the courts should entertain such a case, it is doubtful that such sweeping claims of power as the State Department has made in connection with Vietnam would be upheld.

A much stronger case, however, can be made for the proposition that Congress *has* authorized our military operations in Vietnam, even though there has been no formal declaration of war. In the very same case in which he attributed "the whole powers of war" to Congress, Marshall recognized that by a series of statutes Congress had authorized "limited hostilities" against France, in the so-called "undeclared war" of 1798–1800.

There are a number of Congressional actions that

might be cited to the same effect in connection with the Vietnam war. First and foremost is the Southeast Asia Resolution (better known as the Tonkin Resolution), taken in conjunction with the SEATO treaty. The latter provides that each party to it* "recognizes that aggression by means of armed attack . . . against any of the parties or against any state or territory which the parties by unanimous consent may hereafter designate, would endanger its own peace and safety, and agrees that it will in that event act to meet the common danger in accordance with its constitutional processes." A protocol to the treaty designated Vietnam (also Cambodia and Laos) as within the protection of the quoted clause. The Tonkin Resolution, enacted in August, 1964, approved the President's "determination . . . to take all necessary measures to repel any armed attack against the forces of the United States and to prevent further aggression," and declared that "the United States is . . . prepared, as the President determines, to take all necessary steps, including the use of armed force, to assist any member or protocol state of the Southeast Asia Collective Defense Treaty requesting assistance in defense of its freedom."

Even those who most sharply dispute the constitutional validity of the Vietnam war concede that this language pretty well covers subsequent military actions in Vietnam. But the actual intent and legitimate effect of the Tonkin Resolution are

---

* The parties to the Southeast Asia Collective Defense Treaty, signed Sept. 8, 1954 at Manila, are Australia, France, New Zealand, Pakistan, Philippines, Thailand, the United Kingdom and the United States.

hotly controversial questions today, and its original Congressional sponsors stoutly deny that it was intended to authorize warfare limited only by the President's discretion. However, a few months later, and after the bombing of North Vietnam had begun, Congress approved military appropriations that the Administration explicitly labeled for support of the Vietnam operations. Again and again since, Congress has appropriated the funds requested by the executive for this purpose, and there have been other actions that seemingly conveyed approval of the Vietnam venture, such as the 1965 penalties for the destruction of draft cards, and the 1967 extension of the Selective Service Act.

But if all this makes a strong case it is still a debatable one, and there remains the question whether the courts should undertake to settle it. There is no doubt but that these issues of Presidential power and legislative intent are much much more familiar and congenial to the judicial process than those involving the Nuremberg principles. Furthermore, they are issues arising under the Constitution, the meaning and application of which are normally matters for the courts. But there is serious question whether these particular constitutional issues—involving war, foreign affairs, and the respective powers of the executive and legislative branches—do not fall within a category that the courts have declined to adjudicate, under what lawyers call the "political question doctrine."

An early and leading case illustrating this doctrine occurred in 1849, following a time of chaos in Rhode Island politics when there were two rival state governments. The Constitution provides that "The United States shall guarantee to every State in this Union a Republican form of Government," and it was asserted that one of the two contenders did not meet this requirement and was therefore illegitimate. But the Supreme Court declined to decide the point, on the ground that the question was, as Chief Justice Taney put it, "political in its nature," and thus committed entirely to Congress for decision.[11]

The political question doctrine is itself controversial, and constitutional lawyers do not agree on its nature and purpose. For Herbert Wechsler it is itself a matter of constitutional interpretation; it is finding in the words of the Constitution a direction that a particular provision, or area of governmental action, is removed from the judicial purview and committed exclusively to the legislative or executive branches. For Alexander Bickel, on the other hand, the doctrine is one of judicial discretion, to enable the Supreme Court "to maintain itself in the tension between principle and expediency."[12] Adherents of the Bickel view lay stress on the inherent political weakness of the Federal judiciary, dependent as it is on Congress for organization, jurisdiction and funding, and on the executive for appointments and enforcement of its orders. The courts' survival and ability to make their decisions "stick" depend heavily on public respect for and acceptance of their decisions, and there are occasions when political discretion suggests that the courts do well to stay clear of involvement in divisive and potentially explosive public controversies.

As a theory of constitutional interpretation the Wechsler view is much the more satisfactory, but it may well be that the Bickel approach more accurately reflects the workings of the judges' minds. Certainly there has been ebb and flow in the political question doctrine's application, depending on the temper of the Supreme Court and its disposition to venture into new areas in a spirit of "activism." For many years the late Justice Felix Frankfurter was the leading spokesman of the school of judicial abstention or, as its opponents would call it, abdication. In 1962 his views suffered a sharp setback when the Court, after numerous refusals, finally decided to review the constitutional validity of the structuring of election districts.[13] Many lawyers regard that case as signalling the decline of the political question doctrine, and a greater willingness on the Court's part to step into the breach.

Foreign relations and war-making, however, have long been regarded by the Supreme Court as beyond the judicial ken. "The conduct of the foreign relations of our Government is committed by the Constitution to the Executive and Legislative—'the political'—Departments of Government," wrote Justice Clarke in 1918, "and the propriety of what may be done in the exercise of this political power is not subject to judicial inquiry or decision." More recently the late Justice Jackson, in a case where Supreme Court review of an American war crimes trial was sought, wrote: "Certainly it is not the function of the Judiciary to entertain private litigation —even by a citizen—which challenges the legality, the wisdom, or the propriety of the Commander-in-

Chief in sending our armed forces abroad or to any particular region."[14]

Today the indications are that these views still prevail with a majority of the Supreme Court. In 1966, three Army privates ordered to Vietnam sued to restrain the Army from shipping them out, on the ground that there had been no constitutionally sufficient authorization for American military activity in Vietnam. The lower Federal courts dismissed the suit, and the Supreme Court declined to review that decision by the procedure known as "denial of certiorari."[15] This is a wholly discretionary process by which the Court indicates only that it does not wish to hear a case, without passing on any of the issues it presents. Justices Douglas and Stewart (an odd couple) dissented, saying that the Court should have heard argument, but did not indicate whether they thought the Court should decide the issue of the war's "validity" or, if so, how it should be settled.

This is inconclusive, but certainly suggests no eagerness on the part of the Court to grasp the nettle by telling Congress what it has or has not done, or the President whether he is acting within his constitutional powers. Of course, if a lower Federal court should decide that our Vietnam involvement is unconstitutional, and that therefore the objecting registrant cannot be inducted or the soldier sent to war, the Court might well feel obliged to review the case, rather than let so portentous a ruling stand. But so far that has not happened; the lower courts have held the political doctrine applicable, on the basis of reasons such as those relied on by Judge Charles Wyzanski of the Federal District bench in Massachusetts:

> *From the foregoing this Court concludes that the distinction between a declaration of war and a cooperative action by the legislative and executive with respect to military activities in foreign countries is the very essence of what is meant by a political question. It involves just the sort of evidence, policy considerations, and constitutional principles which elude the normal processes of the judiciary and which are far more suitable for determination by coordinate branches of the government. It is not an act of abdication when a court says that political questions of this sort are not within its jurisdiction. It is a recognition that the tools with which a court can work, the data which it can fairly appraise, the conclusions which it can reach as a basis for entering judgments, have limits.*[16]

As matters stand today, it appears unlikely that the Supreme Court will confront the issue. Still these arguments continue to be pressed in a multitude of lower Federal court cases. Whether or not this is a fruitful technique for resolution of the Vietnam crisis is a question to which I will shortly recur.

Issues such as those just discussed can be determined largely within the framework of United States domestic law, but of course that is not true of the so-called "Nuremberg defense," which rests

113

on over-riding principles of international law and treaties. In another recent case, wherein a draft registrant was convicted of failing to report for induction, the defendant unsuccessfully appealed on the ground that the war is illegal under the London Charter establishing the Nuremberg Tribunal. In this case, too, the Supreme Court declined to review the case, with Justice Douglas the lone dissenter.[17] Supposing that the Court had taken the case, what "law" could it have looked to as the basis of decision?

On this point, the Supreme Court and all other American courts are governed by the so-called "supremacy clause" in Article VI of the Constitution, which provides:

> *This Constitution, and the Laws of the United States which shall be made in Pursuance thereof; and all Treaties made, or which shall be made, under the Authority of the United States, shall be the supreme Law of the Land; and the Judges in every State shall be bound thereby, any Thing in the Constitution or laws of any State to the Contrary notwithstanding.*

For present purposes, the most significant thing about this clause is that international law, except as embodied in treaties to which we are party, is not part of the "supreme law of the land." The second and almost equally important point is that treaties are not accorded any higher dignity than the "laws"—that is, the statutes enacted by Congress. Treaties and statutes stand on an equal footing, and it has long been settled that in the event of conflict or inconsistency between a treaty and a statute, whichever is of later date prevails.[18]

The consequences of all this, as applied to a Supreme Court adjudication of a challenge to the Vietnam operations on "Nuremberg" grounds, is that the Court would have no authority, under the supremacy clause, to rely on doctrines of "just and unjust wars" or any other general international law principles. The Court could look only to treaties, and since the London Charter was never consented to by the Senate, it may not be a "treaty" within the meaning of the supremacy clause, though that is far from clear. Opponents of the war would have to place primary reliance on Article 2 of the United Nations Charter, under which the members agree to "refrain in their international relations from the threat or use of force against the territorial integrity or political independence of any state, or in any other manner inconsistent with the purposes of the United Nations." Supporters of our Vietnam policy would reply by reference to Article 51 of the Charter, which preserves "the inherent right of individual or collective self-defense if an armed attack occurs against a Member of the United Nations."

However, interpretation of the United Nations Charter would not end the matter, because of the parity of treaties and statutes. And here the issue would closely parallel the one just discussed concerning the constitutional basis of our Vietnam operations, for if Congress, by the Tonkin Resolution, appropriations, Selective Service legislation, or in any other statutory way has authorized those activities, these later statutory enactments would prevail in the event of any conflict with the United Nations or London Charters.

The Constitution, of course, is superior to both statutes and treaties. It is conceivable that, in some unlikely contexts, an argument could be made that the Fifth Amendment, in barring Congress from enacting any statute that deprives any "person" of "life, liberty, or property, without due process of law," might be held to embody basic elements of natural law. If in a fit of frenzy Congress should authorize the torture and execution of all prisoners of war, a constitutional barrier might thus be discovered. But it is quite beyond the bounds of possibility that the Court would use so blunt a tool to unravel the tangle of treaties, agreements and resolutions that are involved in determining the aggressive or defensive character of our Vietnam involvement.

In short, under the limitations of the supremacy clause, the Supreme Court *is not authorized* to render judgment on the validity of our participation in the Vietnam war under the Nuremberg principles or international law in general.

The direction in which the foregoing legal factors all point, I believe, is that the courts are not a suitable or sufficient forum for the settlement of our Vietnam problem. And apart from purely legal considerations, it seems to me that there are powerful political and practical considerations that lead to the same conclusion.

Contemplate, for example, the spectacle of the Supreme Court reviewing and pronouncing judgment on the question whether Congress has authorized our Vietnam operations, with Congress sitting at hardly a stone's throw and able to speak for itself. It is true that the Court made just such an adjudication in the steel seizure case, but there the arguments for finding Congressional approval were insubstantial compared to those that can be marshaled in connection with Vietnam. The steel seizure was a single Presidential act, important but paling into insignificance in comparison with the third costliest war in the nation's history, in the conduct of which the Congress has participated in many ways.

Of course, the fact that Congress has not said "no" is not *legally* significant, since the question is whether the war can be constitutionally waged if Congress has not said "yes." But politically, Congress' failure to act decisively to bring the war to an end is exceedingly significant in assessing the consequences of an adverse decision by the Court. As John Norton Moore remarks, "It is difficult for a President to pursue sustained military actions without the active support of a substantial segment of Congress and the American people." Through its power of the purse, its power to make rules for the regulation of the armed forces and if necessary its impeachment powers, a Congress determined to bring the Vietnam war to the quickest possible end can find ways and means to do so. After five years of bloody and costly war sustained by Congressional appropriations, if the President's course is to be checked by another branch of the Government, it is the Congress and not the Court that can and should be the checking agent.

Quite apart from the limitations of the supremacy clause, the objections to a Court decision based on the anti-aggression provisions of the Nuremberg or United Nations Charters are even more compelling. The political strain on the Court would be much greater, for while a decision on the constitutional basis of the war would appear as a sort of judicial arbitration between the two other branches' respective powers, a decision based on the Nuremberg principles would be regarded as putting international law over Constitution, Congress and President combined.

Furthermore, the evidentiary problems would be well-nigh insuperable. It is hardly to be thought that the United States and South Vietnamese governments would open up their secret diplomatic and military document files for inspection by the litigants. At Nuremberg and Tokyo alike, military conquest had accomplished just that, and especially at Nuremberg the volume and candor of the documents, as well as Hitler's focal role, greatly simplified the issue of intent.

But no such aids are available now. "An international lawyer writing about an ongoing war cannot hope to reach clear conclusions about all the legal issues involved," writes Richard Falk: "It is virtually impossible to unravel conflicting facts underlying conflicting legal claims."[19] An American court, be it the Supreme Court or a lesser tribunal, would find the path to "clear conclusions" equally obstructed. Total military victories such as those that ended the Second World War are comparatively rare in modern history, and it is difficult to envisage other circumstances that would unlock the secret files. In the nuclear age, with the three greatest powers involved in the Vietnam war, total victory would probably leave few with any stomach for war crimes trials, or indeed any stomachs at all.

In some draft resistance cases, the defendants have pressed the "Nuremberg defense" by contending that, if the Vietnam war is in fact aggressive, they will be liable to prosecution as war criminals if they engage in it. Professor Falk has given this argument a qualified blessing, writing that "the wider logic of Nuremberg extends to embrace all those who, knowingly at any rate, participate in a war they have reason to believe violates the restraints of international law."[20]

Wherever the "wider logic" might lead, the Nuremberg judgments, as we have seen, have no such wide embrace. Those convicted at both Nuremberg and Tokyo of "crimes against peace" were all part of the inner circles of leadership, and the Nuremberg acquittals of generals and industrialists cut directly against Professor Falk's argument. Furthermore, there is much ambiguity in his phrase "reason to believe." No doubt there are today millions of Americans who, on the basis of generally available information, would claim a "reasonable belief" that we are "in the wrong" in Vietnam and, if educated in the terminology, would label it "aggressive." But there are more millions who think otherwise, and the issue between these disagreeing millions cannot rationally be projected in terms of criminal liability for rendering military service.

"There was no decision in Nuremberg," writes Benjamin Ferencz, one of the prosecutors there, "which would support a conclusion that the United

States Armed Forces, like pirate ships, are criminal organizations."[21] Nor was there any decision that international law confers immunity from military service on the basis of an individual's personal judgment that his country's foreign and military policies are wrong. Much less was it decided that domestic courts can be expected to sit in judgment on the foreign policies of the very government of which those courts are a part. The Nuremberg and Tokyo judgments were rendered by international tribunals on a *post mortem* basis (all too literally), surrounded by virtual libraries of the defeated governments' most secret papers. Professor Falk overlooks these factors, I believe, in suggesting that domestic courts sitting during the course of hostilities may be called upon to follow in the footsteps of Nuremberg, let alone embrace its "wider logic."

Lawyers called upon to represent young men who refuse to serve are abundantly justified in raising both the constitutional and the Nuremberg arguments in their defense. The force and sincerity of such contentions may serve their clients well even if they do not prevail as propositions of law. Judges and juries should be made aware of the tenuous basis on which they are asked to attribute criminal guilt to men whose driving motive may be that of obedience to a higher law. Furthermore, these arguments based on constitutional or international principle are of great public benefit in projecting profound moral and political issues in the legal dimension and expanding public understanding of our national predicament.

But the predicament itself is not, I believe, susceptible to solution by judicial decree. There is no such simple way to end the Vietnam tragedy, for the Supreme Court is not a *deus ex machina*. This war, and the agony and rancor that are its product, have been the work of the President and the Congress—the people's elected agents—and the war can be ended only by action of the national will, exerted through political, not judicial, channels.

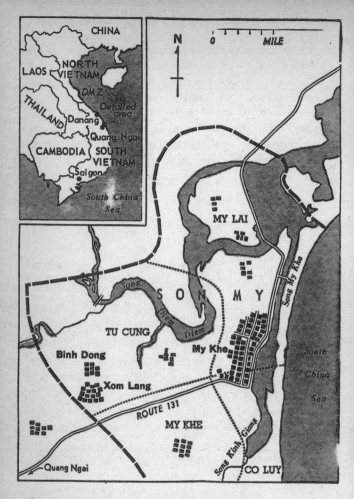

Son My, nominally a "village" but in fact more like an American township, contained four "hamlets," of which one was called My Lai. But the killings took place principally in the sub-hamlets Xom Lang and Binh Dong in the hamlet Tu Cung. Xom Lang, the scene of the initial American strike, was erroneously labelled My Lai (4) on American maps of the area. The name "Pinkville," much used in the press, arose because on American maps populated areas were colored pink.

# 6 / War Crimes: Son My

"MILITARY OPERATIONS . . . swelled in size and savagery. Against the stubborn guerrilla warfare . . . the U.S. Army poured in regiments, brigades, divisions. . . . [The enemy] burned, ambushed, raided, mutilated; on occasion they buried prisoners alive. Americans retaliated with atrocities of their own, burning down a whole village and killing every inhabitant if an American soldier was found with his throat cut, applying the 'water cure' and other tortures to obtain information. They were three thousand miles from home, exasperated by heat, malaria, tropical rains, mud and mosquitoes . . . and officers on occasion issued orders to take no more prisoners."

South Vietnam 1967–1968? No—the Philippines, 1899–1900, as described by Barbara Tuchman.[1] Her account of the reaction to the suppression of the Philippine "insurrection" that accompanied our annexation of those islands is an extraordinary reverse *déja vu* of the current crisis of feeling about the Vietnam war and the way it is being waged.

## Eyewitness Account . . .

*Eyewitness account of the killing of Jews by German SS-men on Oct. 5, 1942, at Dubno in Ukrainia (U.S.S.R.), from an affidavit by Hermann G. Graebe, a German construction-engineer, Nuremberg Document 2922-PS.*

I drove to the site . . . and saw near it great mounds of earth, about 30 meters long and 2 meters high. Several trucks stood in front of the mounds. Armed Ukrainian militia drove the people off the trucks under the supervision of an SS-man. The militia men acted as guards on the trucks and drove them to and from the pit. All these people had the regulation yellow patches on the front and back of their clothes, and thus could be recognized as Jews . . .

I walked around the mound, and found myself confronted by a tremendous grave. People were closely wedged together and lying on top of each other so that only their heads were visible. Nearly all had blood running over their shoulders from their heads. Some of the people shot were still moving. Some were lifting their arms and turning their heads to show that they were still alive. The pit was already two-thirds full. I estimated that it already contained about 1,000 people. I looked for the man who did the shooting. He was an SS-man, who sat at the edge of the narrow end of the pit, his feet dangling into the pit. He had a tommy gun on his knees and was smoking a cigarette. The people, completely naked, went down some steps which were cut in the clay wall of the pit and clambered over the heads of the people lying there to the place to which the SS-man directed them. They lay down in front of the dead or injured people; some caressed those who were still alive and spoke to them in a low voice. Then I heard a series of shots. I looked into the pit and saw that the bodies were twitching or the heads lying already motionless on top of the bodies that lay before them. Blood was running from their necks. I was surprised that I was not ordered away, but I saw that there were two or three postmen in uniform nearby. The next batch was approaching already. They went down into the pit, lined themselves up against the previous victims and were shot. When I walked back, round the mound I noticed another truckload of people which had just arrived. This time it included sick and infirm people.

## . . . From Two Wars

*Eyewitness accounts of the killings in Son My, as reported by Richard Hammer in* One Morning in the War *(1970), pp. 135-36.*

Led by a group of GI's, Pham Phon, his wife and three small children reached the canal. There, "I saw a lot of people who were grouping there, people were crying, especially babies were crying. But GI's stand on both sides of the canal so nobody . . . can move away."

"Meanwhile," says Phon, "another group of GI's search the next hamlet, the sub-hamlet called Binh Dong, about five hundred meters from my hamlet. And the GI's had other people from this new hamlet. They brought them to the canal. There must have been more than one hundred, but who can count at such a time."

When Phon saw the Americans herding this large group from Binh Dong to the canal, he had a premonition of disaster. And this was reinforced by the sounds of gunfire that he heard from Xom Lang. "I tell my wife and my kids, slip into the canal when GI not looking. We watch for our chance and we do that. So then the GI begin to shoot at the standing people and at the sitting people on the banks of the canal. They fall into the canal and cover us with their bodies. So we were not wounded, myself, my wife and my two sons. My little daughter, only seven years old, she was wounded in the arm when GI's shoot into the canal when they heard the people groaning and making much noise."

Just as the slaughter at the canal began, Richard Roe happened to be passing by. "They had them in a group, standing over a ditch—just like a Nazi-type thing," he remembers. "One officer ordered a kid to machine gun everybody down. But the kid couldn't do it. He threw the machine gun down and the officer picked it up. I don't remember seeing any men in the ditch. Mostly women and kids."

Roe left for another part of the hamlet. Later he returned . . . Roe was at the canal, sitting on a mound eating some chow with John Doe. As they were eating, the two noticed that "some of them were still breathing. They were pretty badly shot up. They weren't going to get any medical help, and so we shot them, shot maybe five of them."

125

What actually happened at Son My (better but inaccurately known as My Lai) in March of 1968 is and may well remain obscured by the fog of war, the passage of time, and the self-interest of surviving participants and observers. Especially in view of the criminal charges pending against a number of those involved, it is no part of the purpose of this book to point the finger of guilt at any individual. Whether the killings constituted a war crime is the question first to be examined and, for this purpose, it can be taken as undisputed that on March 16, 1968, American troops at Son My killed a large number of the village residents of both sexes and all ages. According to President Nixon, who presumably was well briefed: "What appears was certainly a massacre, under no circumstances was it justified. . . . We cannot ever condone or use atrocities against civilians . . ."

Son My is a village in Quang Ngai Province, situated close to the seacoast in the narrow northern neck of South Vietnam, about 100 miles south of the 17th Parallel demarcation line. In 1954, at the time of the partition, thousands of Quang Ngai's inhabitants preferred the Hanoi regime and moved north. In later years many returned as Vietcong organizers; the entire province became a stronghold of the National Liberation Front (NLF),* and Son My village came under Vietcong control in 1964. From time to time there were skirmishes between the Vietcong and the South Vietnamese

---

* The official name of the politico-military organization whose military arm is referred to in the United States as Vietcong, meaning Vietnamese Communist.

(ARVN) units, and in 1967, after the great American build-up, American Army patrols appeared from time to time, but without untoward incident. In January, 1968, the Tet offensive brought severe fighting in the nearby provincial capital of Quang Ngai, but Son My itself did not suffer. By this time, however, a large number of other villages in the province had been destroyed, as a result of American search and destroy operations coupled with extremely heavy air strikes.[2]

The Son My killings took place in the course of a standard type of American military operation in Quang Ngai, the nature of which was a sudden lift of troops by helicopter, in and on all sides of a reported enemy unit, in an attempt to close a trap on it and destroy it. In this instance the operation, under the code name "Muscatine," was carried out by an *ad hoc* unit of three infantry companies, called "Task Force Barker" after its commander, the late Lieut. Col. Frank A. Barker Jr. The parent unit of the task force was the 11th Brigade, which in turn was part of the newly formed Americal Division, commanded by Maj. Gen. Samuel W. Koster.

About mid-March, 1968, the American command received information that a strong Vietcong unit, the 48th Local Force Battalion, was regrouping after the Tet offensive at Son My, in the hamlet of My Lai. Task Force Barker thereupon planned a helicopter operation for March 16, under which one of its three companies would go into My Lai and engage the enemy, while the other two companies would be set down to the north and east of the target, to prevent the Vietcong from escaping the trap.

It appears that there was in fact a Vietcong unit in My Lai, centered in the subhamlet of My Khe, shown on American military maps as My Lai (1). Whether because of linguistic and map confusion or for some other reason, however, the central target of the attack on the morning of March 16 was the subhamlet Xom Lang in the hamlet Tu Cung, labelled My Lai (4) on the American maps, about two miles distant from My Khe where the Vietcong were based.

Consequently, when C Company of Task Force Barker went into Xom Lang that morning, expecting heavy opposition, it encountered none. The company had had little combat experience, and had recently suffered casualties from mines and booby-traps that had enraged and frightened the men; apparently there had been brutal and inexcusable killings of Vietnamese before the assault on Xom Lang.

What happened when the soldiers reached the dwellings is too well-known from newspaper and magazine photographs, and the accounts of numerous participants to warrant repetition.[3] It appears certain that the troops had been told to destroy all the structures and render the place uninhabitable; what they had been told to do with the residents is not so clear. However that may be, the accounts indicate that C Company killed virtually every inhabitant on whom they could lay hands, regardless of age or sex, and despite the fact that no opposition or hostile behavior was encountered. There were few survivors, and based on the prior population of the area, the deaths attributable to C Company in Xom Lang and Binh Dong, together with other killings said to have been perpetrated a few hours later by a platoon of B Company a few miles to the east in the subhamlet My Hoi, amounted to about 500.

There was certainly nothing clandestine about the killings. About 80 officers and men went into the Xom Lang area on the ground. Above them, at various altitudes, were gunship, observation and command helicopters. There was constant radio communication between the various units and their superiors, and these were monitored at brigade headquarters. A reporter and a photographer from an Army Public Information Detachment went in with the troops and witnessed and recorded the course of events virtually from start to finish. The pilot of an observation helicopter, shocked by what he saw, reported the killings to brigade headquarters and repeatedly put his helicopter down to rescue wounded women and children. Command helicopters for the divisional, brigade and task force commanders were assigned air space over the field of action, and were there at least part of the time.

Such were the tragic fruits of Operation Muscatine in the village of Son My. Beyond doubt there were crimes, but were they "war crimes"? The answer to this question is not altogether simple, and neither is it unimportant, as it may bear closely on issues of personal liability, and the authority under which alleged perpetrators may be tried.

The complications arise from the multilateral nature of the Vietnam war and its guerrilla character, marked by the absence of any military "front" dividing the two sides. Directly involved in the fighting are on the one side the North Vietnamese Army and the Vietcong, and on the other the South Vietnamese units and the greatly stronger allied forces of the United States, as well as contingents from South Korea, the Philippines, Thailand, Australia and New Zealand. Until the Cambodian excursion, all of the ground fighting took place on the territory of South Vietnam, but large parts of the country are controlled by the Vietcong, and Son My might well have been regarded as "enemy" territory in that sense at the time of the assault.

With the exception of the NLF, all participants in the conflict are parties to the four Geneva Conventions of 1949, of which the two most important for present purposes are the "Prisoners of War" and "Protection of Civilian Persons in Time of War" conventions. But in June, 1965, when the International Committee of the Red Cross addressed a letter to the four principal belligerents declaring that they were all bound by the 1949 conventions and asking for information concerning the steps being taken to comply with the prisoner-of-war provisions, North Vietnam as well as the NLF declined to acknowledge that they were obligated under the conventions, while declaring that prisoners were being "well treated" (North Vietnam) or "humanely treated" (NLF). And in fact neither of the two has complied with the conventions. North Vietnam in particular has consistently refused to carry out the reporting, correspondence and neutral inspection provisions relating to prisoners of war, and the Vietcong units have commonly disregarded the requirements that combatants shall carry arms openly and "have a fixed distinctive sign recognizable at a distance."

The legal situation is further complicated by the fact that the Geneva Conventions as a whole apply only to "armed conflict . . . between two or more" signatory nations, while Article 3, containing certain "minimum" prohibitions of inhumane treatment of prisoners or civilians, applies also to "armed conflict not of an international character occurring in the territory of" a signatory power.[4] Whether the Vietnamese war is a "civil" or "international" war is one of the points in dispute, and the phrase "international civil war" is nothing but a handy verbal compromise that solves nothing. However that may be, there is no room whatsoever for a North Vietnamese contention that they are not bound at least by Article 3 and, since their regular troops are engaged with those of South Vietnam and its allies in South Vietnamese territory, there appears to be little force in their effort to escape responsibility under the conventions in their entirety. The NLF, as a nonsignatory, is in a much stronger position with respect to the particular provisions of the conventions but, of course, is bound, as is every organized military force claiming or aspiring to sovereignty, by the customary laws of war.

International lawyers have discussed at length whether and to what extent North Vietnam and the NLF are bound by the conventions[5] and, if negative answers are supportable, the question then arises whether South Vietnam and the United States are bound if their opponents are not. The conventions themselves do not say that a signatory's obligation to comply is dependent on reciprocity, and in any event customary law binds the United States as it does the NLF.

But so far as concerns the obligations of the United States, we need not pursue these vexing questions further. Claiming as it does to be an intervenor only to protect South Vietnam against aggression, and to be fighting under the banner of justice and humanity, the United States cannot possibly take the position that her forces are not bound by the laws of war, whether customary or embodied in treaties to which she is signatory. To the credit of our Government, it has made no such claim, and acknowledges that its conduct of military operations, whether against North Vietnamese or Vietcong, is subject to those laws and treaties.

The crucial difficulty is that neither at Son My, nor in most of the other actions charged against our forces, has it been clear that the victims were either North Vietnamese or Vietcong. Indeed, the basis of the charge is that often they are *not*, and that we are indiscriminately killing civilians who may be and often are South Vietnamese innocent of any hostile action against our troops. What laws of war, if any, govern the relations between those troops and the civilian population of South Vietnam?

Before 1949, this question would have been governed by Section III of The Hague Convention of 1907, entitled "Military Authority over the Territory of the Hostile State," and reflecting in the title its basis in the customary laws of war, which apply only between belligerents. The issue would generally be whether the place where the challenged action took place should be regarded as "friendly" territory controlled by our allies, or "enemy" territory controlled by the NLF and to which the laws of war would apply.

The Geneva "Civilian Persons" Convention, however, applies to "all cases of partial or total occupation of the territory of" a signatory, and the persons protected by the convention include "those who, at a given moment . . . find themselves, in the case of a conflict or occupation, in the hands of a Party to the conflict or Occupying Power of which they are not nationals." On their face, these provisions would appear to cover the situation of South Vietnamese nationals who, like the inhabitants of Son My, find themselves "in the hands" of the United States forces, but this is rendered dubious by still another provision, which excludes from the convention's coverage "nationals of a co-belligerent State" which "has normal diplomatic representation in the State in whose hands they are." The theory of this clause is that the inhabitants can rely on normal diplomatic processes for protection against abuse, but it is certainly doubtful whether the South Vietnamese Government is either able or disposed to furnish such protection for its nationals "in the hands of" the United States. On this basis it could be argued that *all* South Vietnamese nationals enjoy the protection of the Geneva Convention *vis-à-vis* the American forces, but this conclusion is by no means clear.

133

If the more conservative view that the laws of war do not apply to American-South Vietnamese relations generally is taken, then one must fall back on the orthodox distinction between "friendly" and "enemy" territory. If an American soldier rapes and murders a South Vietnamese girl in Saigon, it is a crime punishable by court-martial under the articles of war,* but not a war crime. The terrible episode poignantly described by Daniel Lang in "Casualties of War," involving the American patrol that kidnapped a South Vietnamese girl to serve as luggage-carrier and lust-gratifier, and then murdered her, was apparently not a war crime, for the same reasons.[6]

But Son My was in an area regarded as a Vietcong stronghold, and the hamlets assaulted were thought to be Vietcong military bases. The troops went in expecting to encounter resistance, and under orders to destroy the habitations and deal ruthlessly with any resistance. It would be highly artificial to say that this was not "hostile" territory within the meaning of The Hague Convention, or to question the applicability of the laws of war to the events of March 16, 1968, at Son My. What, then, were the applicable laws?

The presence of infants and the aged, as well as many women, among those killed at Son My underlined the horror of the episode, but is not directly relevant to the legality of what was done. It is sad but true that the weak and helpless are not exempt

---

* The crime would also be punishable under Vietnamese law, but Americans in South Vietnam, under the applicable assistance treaties, are immune from Vietnamese criminal process.

from the scourge of war. Indeed, they are likely to be the first to succumb to the starvation and other deprivations that are the consequence and, indeed, the purpose of an economic blockade. In this day and age they are at least as often the victims of aerial bombardment as are regular troops. The death of an infant in consequence of military operations, therefore, does not establish that a war crime has been committed.

All this is as true in Vietnam as in any other war. Furthermore, in Vietnam the weaker inhabitants are not only victims, but often also participants. It is not necessary to be a male, or particularly strong, to make a booby-trap, plant a mine, or toss a hand grenade a few yards. American soldiers are often the losers in these lethal little games played by those who appear helpless and inoffensive. Furthermore, these actions are not occasional aberrations; on the contrary, they are basic features of Vietcong strategy. As the leading military figure of North Vietnam, General Vo Nguyen Giap, has put it:

> The protracted popular war in Vietnam demanded . . . appropriate forms of combat: appropriate for the revolutionary nature of the war in relation to the balance of forces then showing a clear enemy superiority. . . . The form of combat adopted was guerrilla warfare . . . each inhabitant a soldier; each village a fortress. . . . The entire population participates in the armed struggle, fighting, according to the principles of guerrilla warfare, in small units. . . . This is the fundamental content of the war of people.[7]

135

Now, guerrilla warfare is not intrinsically unlawful, but as waged by the Vietcong it is undeniably in violation of the traditional laws of war and the Geneva Conventions, based as they are on the distinction between combatants and noncombatants. Combatants need not wear uniforms (which the North Vietnamese generally do) but must observe the conventional four requirements: to be commanded "by a person responsible for his subordinates"; to wear "a fixed distinctive emblem recognizable at a distance"; to "carry arms openly"; and to "conduct their operations in accordance with the laws and customs of war." The Vietcong commonly disregard at least the second and third provisions, and in response to the Red Cross inquiry, declared that they were *not* bound by the Geneva Conventions, on the grounds that they were not signatories and that the conventions contained provisions unsuited to their "action" and their "organization . . . of armed forces."

Like a spy, a guerrilla may be a hero, but if he engages in combat without observing the requirements, he violates the laws of war and is subject to punishment, which may be the death penalty. Nor is there any special court for juveniles; the small boy who throws a grenade is as "guilty" as the able-bodied male of military age. This may seem a harsh rule, but it is certainly the law, and its continuing validity was reaffirmed in several of the Nuremberg trials. As one of the tribunals put the matter:

> *We think the rule is established that a civilian who aids, abets, or participates in the fighting*

*is liable to punishment as a war criminal under
the rules of war. Fighting is legitimate only for
the combatant personnel. . . . It is only this
group that is entitled to treatment as prisoners
of war and incurs no liability beyond detention
after capture or surrender.*[8]

However, Richard Falk and other international
lawyers have strongly pressed the argument that an
insurgent revolutionary movement cannot possibly
comply with the rules for the identification of combatants, or other laws of war, especially when con-
fronting a foe so vastly superior in mobility and firepower as the United States. "I would suggest," Falk
writes, "that the insurgent faction in an undeveloped
country has, at the beginning of its struggle for
power, no alternative other than terror to mobilize
an effective operation."[9]

This is, of course, the familiar argument of "military necessity" which we have already examined.
If emblems and the other indicia of combatant
status are to be discarded and the whole population engaged in combat, as Giap describes, then the
same argument of necessity may justify the power
against whom this type of war is directed in resorting to hitherto unlawful means to counter the guerrilla forces. As will shortly appear, this point may
have some relevance to the lawfulness of the population transfers and "free-fire zones" that have become a common feature of our military policy in
Vietnam.

But however far the "necessity" argument be
stretched, it cannot justify what was done at Son

My. Given the history and location of the village, the Americans might have had reason to suspect that many of the inhabitants were sympathetic to the Vietcong. There has been no suggestion, however, that there was reason to believe that any particular individual had engaged in hostile conduct. Even had there been such grounds, the slaughter of all the inhabitants would have been an unlawful and atrocious reaction; the Geneva Conventions are explicit that persons suspected of violating the laws of war shall "be treated with humanity" and not punished without trial and opportunity to contest the charge. And while small boys can toss grenades, infants in arms cannot, and were nonetheless killed along with the rest.

Painfully anticipatory of Son My was an action of German troops during the occupation of Greece, described in the Nuremberg tribunal's judgment in the so-called "Hostage case":

> On 5 April 1944, the notorious "blood bath" at Klissura occurred. The facts are: On the date in question an engagement between [guerrilla] bands and German troops occurred about 2½ kilometers outside the village of Klissura. After the retreat of the bands, the troops moved into the village and began searching for evidence of band support. None was found. Later in the afternoon, units of the 7th SS Panzer Grenadier Regiment entered the village and began almost immediately to kill the inhabitants. At least 215 persons, and undoubtedly more, were

*killed. Among those killed were 9 children less than 1 year old, 6 between 1 and 2 years of age, 8 between 2 and 3 years, and 4 between 4 and 5 years. There were 72 massacred who were less than 15 years of age, and 7 people in excess of 80 years. No justification existed for this outrage. It was plain murder.*[10]

On the basis of this and other episodes involving troops under his command, and his "indifference to these unjustified and brutal murders," General Helmuth Felmy was sentenced to a 15-year prison term. The three-member tribunal comprised judges of the Supreme Courts of Iowa and Nebraska, and a Michigan attorney who had served on the United States Supreme Court's Advisory Committee on Rules of Criminal Procedure.

I have dealt with the Son My killings at length because of the scale of the disaster, the extensive though belated publicity it has received, and the fact that it is the only mass killing of the Vietnam war that our Government has acknowledged as a crime. It has been said that "the massacre at Son My was not unique,"[11] but I am unaware of any evidence of other incidents of comparable magnitude, and the reported reaction of some of the soldiers at Son My strongly indicates that they regarded it as out of the ordinary. There have, however, been numerous indications that our troops have killed many other civilians under parallel circumstances, and equally in violation of the laws of war. Obviously, this state of affairs poses questions far more searching than the criminal liability of the soldiers who did the shooting at Son My.

In February, 1965, the United States began a program of aerial bombardment of targets in North Vietnam that lasted, with interruptions, until President Johnson announced its cessation in the famous television address declaring that he would not seek re-election. From the start the North Vietnamese branded the raids unlawful, and during 1965 and 1966 repeatedly threatened to try captured American pilots as war criminals under the Nuremberg precedents.

Home-grown critics have been almost equally sharp; Lt. Gen. James Gavin, for one, described the bombing as "militarily unsound and morally wrong." Whether or not the bombing of North Vietnam was "militarily unsound" is a debatable but not a legal issue, and General Gavin did not make it clear whether he believed the attacks to be "morally wrong" *because* "militarily unsound," or whether he would regard them as morally reprehensible even if militarily effective. Nor did the North Vietnamese go beyond a general invocation of "Nuremberg" to clarify the basis of their threatened criminal charges against the pilots.

In fact, as already remarked, the Nuremberg and Tokyo judgments are silent on the subject of aerial bombardment. Whatever may have been the laws of war before the Second World War, by the time the war ended there was not much law left. Since both sides had played the terrible game of urban destruction—the Allies far more successfully—there was no basis for criminal charges against Germans or Japanese, and in fact no such charges were brought.*

In the winter of 1966, Harrison Salisbury's reports from North Vietnam raised a storm of criticism of our bombing. In retrospect, this marked public reaction seems more significant than the content of his dispatches which, while graphically describing the extent of the physical damage, fell far short of demonstrating any intent to cause civilian casualties. After the experience of the Second World War one might have supposed it to be common knowledge that heavy bombing near populated areas—even if strictly military objectives are targeted—inevitably kills people and destroys their dwellings. That Salisbury's reports came as such a shock can only be explained by forgetfulness and wishful thinking, fostered by benighted Pentagon publicity that sought to convey that our bombs are destructive of North Vietnamese bridges, factories, and gunsites, but harmless to human beings.

Others who have visited North Vietnam have remarked on the prevalence of bomb damage in rural areas apparently remote from any worthwhile

---

* In consequence of a curious course of history, only Japanese courts have ever considered the legality of aerial bombardment. In Aug., 1942, apparently in reaction to Gen. James Doolittle's famous carrier-launched raid over Japan the previous April, Japan passed a law for the punishment of enemy aviators who bombed illegal targets. A number of Doolittle's flyers were captured by the Japanese, and executed pursuant to this law. The trials appear to have been *pro forma*, and after the war several Japanese officers were convicted by the Americans of war crimes in that they had executed the pilots without a *bona fide* trial.

In 1963, a Tokyo civil court rendered judgment in a suit for damages brought by survivors of the Hiroshima and Nagasaki bombings. The court denied recovery, but characterized the atomic bombings as "contrary to the fundamental principles of the laws of war."[12]

targets, and reported the use of antipersonnel bombs. It is difficult to assess these strictures. Antipersonnel bombs would be suitable for use against gunsites or other military locations. Things do not look the same from a jet bomber as they do on the ground, and the possibility of error is very great. Given the state of aerial warfare to which we were brought by the Second World War, in any event, I can see no sufficient basis for war crimes charges based on the bombing of North Vietnam. Whatever the laws of war in this field *ought* to be, certainly Nuremberg furnishes no basis for these accusations.

If the silence of Nuremberg answers no questions about what "ought" to be the law, it certainly asks them, and these unanswered questions are especially relevant to American bombing policies not in the North, but in South Vietnam.

Is there any significant difference between killing a babe-in-arms by a bomb dropped from a high-flying aircraft, or by an infantryman's point-blank gunfire? As we have seen, by common practice of the antagonists in the Second World War massive aerial bombardment of population centers, for the purpose of destroying habitations and killing or terrorizing the population, became an accepted part of "strategic air warfare." If that is to be tolerated under the customary law of war, would that have justified Allied ground forces in entering German and Japanese towns with guns blazing, and killing off the infants who survived the bombing? Few would support such a proposition, but the distinction is seldom articulated other than by describing the aviator's act as more "impersonal" than the ground soldier's.

This may be psychologically valid, but surely is not morally satisfactory. The answer, if there is one, must be found in a rule of reason, closely related to military necessity. The Allied aviator over Berlin and the infantryman occupying a German town were in quite different situations. The aviator was attacking a functioning part of the German war machine with a weapon that could not discriminate among those in the target area, any more than could the captain of a ship participating in a naval blockade. The soldier was part of a force occupying conquered territory, and was in a position to observe and discriminate among the inhabitants and fulfill his military functions without shooting babes-in-arms.

An important ingredient of this principle of reason and necessity is proportion: The military end sought should be sufficient to warrant the suffering and destruction inflicted. To a degree this rule of proportion was observed during the Second World War. Oxford and Cambridge were not bombed; neither was Heidelberg, and it is a terrible memory that we did not stay our hand at Dresden, when the war was as good as won. The rights and wrongs of Hiroshima are debatable, but I have never heard a plausible justification of Nagasaki. It is difficult to contest the judgment that Dresden and Nagasaki were war crimes, tolerable in retrospect only because their malignancy pales in comparison to Dachau, Auschwitz and Treblinka.

143

These reflections have taken us away from Vietnam where, despite the enormous tonnage of bombs dropped, there have been no urban holocausts. The massive bombardments by the B-52's have been mainly in rural and wooded areas, directed against suspected enemy troop concentrations. But in South Vietnam there has been a great deal of aerial activity on our part which does not fit this pattern at all, and that comes much closer to the situation of the ground soldier. Indeed, most of these aerial actions are carried out in close concert with ground forces, and are part of a single joint operation.

A great many of these actions involve the destruction of hamlets from which a sniper bullet has been fired, or a shot has been fired at an American helicopter, or near which a mine or booby trap has exploded, or even which are merely suspected of having harbored Vietcong. A United States Marine Corps "Ultimatum to Vietnamese People" declared that "The U.S. Marines will not hesitate to destroy immediately, any village or hamlet harboring the Vietcong," and another Marine leaflet informed the inhabitants that their village "was bombed because you harbored Vietcong" and "will be bombed again if you harbor Vietcong in any way."

The by now voluminous reportorial literature on the Vietnamese war leaves little doubt that air strikes are routinely directed against hamlets and even single habitations on the basis described above, in reliance on information of varying reliability. Obviously, these tactics are a response to the nature of guerrilla warfare, and the difficulty of sifting out the "enemy" in a society where there are many shades of inimical activity, and friend and foe are not readily distinguishable. Making full allowance for these difficulties, however, it is clear that such reprisal attacks are a flagrant violation of the Geneva Convention on Civilian Protection, which prohibits "collective penalties" and "reprisals against protected persons," and equally in violation of the Rules of Land Warfare.[13] Son My, after all, was suspected of harboring the Vietcong, and if (as has been seen) it was nonetheless a war crime to round up the inhabitants and shoot them without trial, it would be equally criminal to have killed them by a surprise air attack.

Even more ominous problems are created by the so-called "free-fire" (artillery) or "free-strike" (air) zones that have been a frequent means of dealing with the guerrilla problem. The basic theory of this technique is that since the guerrillas live among the rural population and are difficult to distinguish, the thing to do is to remove the rural population, leaving the Vietcong isolated and exposed. Proponents of the technique often refer to Mao Tse-tung's figure of speech about guerrillas as fish, and the people as the water in which the fish swim. To catch the fish, remove the water. Q.E.D.

The method of these operations is to select an area where the Vietcong are thought to be strong, and saturate it with ground troops brought in by helicopter, with strong air support. The villagers are evacuated to refugee camps, more or less forcefully, and the homes, livestock, and all useful appurtenances destroyed, so as to render the area at least temporarily uninhabitable. Thereafter the entire area is declared a "free-fire" zone of operations, wherein people or things can be fired upon at will and discretion, and without prior warning, or clearance from the Vietnamese provincial authorities.

Now there is enough question about the legality of the evacuation procedures alone to give pause, for Article 49 of the Geneva Convention prohibits "individual or mass forcible transfers, as well as deportations of protected persons from occupied territory to the territory of the Occupying Power." To be sure it is doubtful, as we have seen, whether this article applies to relations between the United States and the South Vietnamese civilian population. Likewise, the evacuations are generally conducted with the approval of the Saigon Government. And finally, Article 49 goes on to authorize "total or partial evacuation of a given area if the security of the population or imperative military reasons so demand."

Nevertheless, serious questions remain, for it is not at all clear whether the clause just quoted was intended to justify population transfers of this type, in which devastation of the evacuated area is the prime objective. "Persons thus evacuated," the article elsewhere provides, "shall be transferred back to their homes as soon as hostilities in the area in question have ceased," but in South Vietnam generally the homes will have been destroyed. Furthermore, it is required that: "The Occupying Power undertaking such transfers or evacuations shall ensure, to the greatest practicable extent, that proper accommodation is provided to receive the protected persons, that the removals are effected in satisfactory conditions of hygiene, health, safety and nutrition, and that members of the same family are not separated." It is common knowledge that the record of fulfillment of our obligations to the refugees we have, in military parlance, "generated," has been shockingly inadequate. Samuel P. Huntington estimated that one and a half million refugees have passed through the camps, where conditions "have at times been horrendous."[14] Jonathan Schell observed the devastation of a "free-fire" zone of some 200 square kilometers where 17,000 people were living, by means of an operation which "was not supposed to generate any new refugees" because no camps were available.[15]

If the legality of the population transfer program remains a doubtful proposition, that can hardly be said of the "free firing" and the air strikes carried out in the zone so created. "In the mountains, just about anything that moves is considered to be V.C.," an Air Force major told Jonathan Schell: "We've cleared most of the people out of there, and anything that's left has got to be V.C." And so helicopters and small observation planes go "squirrel-hunting" for individuals observed in the devastated areas, using machine-guns from the helicopters, and calling in air strikes—"sniping with bombs." This is using the aircraft for the same purposes that the infantry man uses his gun, and the pilot ought to be held to the same standards of distinguishing combatants from noncombatants. Realizing this, the pilots claim extraordinary powers of divination, professing ability to "spot the V.C."

147

by the fact that he runs away, or "walks real proud, with a kind of bounce in his gait, like a soldier, instead of just shuffling along, like the farmers do," or occupies a "hootch" among the trees rather than in the open. Perhaps the pilots are more often right than wrong, but this certainly is not the method for dealing with civilians suspected of hostile activity which is required by the laws of war, and is unlawful for the same reasons that the Son My killings were unlawful.

Still another aspect of our conduct in Vietnam that raises serious questions under the laws of war is our handling of prisoners. Until recently this matter appeared to be one of vicarious responsibility for mistreatment by the South Vietnamese of prisoners turned over to them by the American forces. In the spring of 1970, however, the court-martial proceedings against Lieut. James B. Duffy disclosed distressing indications that American practice with regard to prisoners may be degenerating.

This is, to be sure, an area where the enemy has given great provocation. Both North Vietnam and the NLF have repudiated the Geneva Conventions. Neither has complied with the requirements of customary law with respect to notifications and correspondence. There have been many reports of brutal treatment of American captives, and authenticated reports in 1966 and 1967 that the North Vietnamese paraded American pilots through the streets of Hanoi, in violation of the Geneva injunction against subjecting prisoners to "insults and public curiosity." Much worse, in 1965 the NLF announced the execution of three American prisoners, in reprisal for South Vietnamese executions of several Vietcong "terrorists." Reprisals against prisoners of war were prohibited by the 1929 Geneva Convention, and are forbidden today under both the 1949 Convention and the American Army's Law of Land Warfare.[16]

These open violations on the part of the enemy may well have inclined the American authorities to turn a blind eye to the numerous reports of South Vietnamese torture and general mistreatment of prisoners that have persisted throughout the course of the war. To be sure, the United States is not legally responsible for what South Vietnam does with its own prisoners, but the matter is of importance because the American forces do not retain permanent custody of the prisoners they take, but send them to rear-area camps maintained by the South Vietnamese.

Article 12 of the Geneva Convention authorizes such transfers, but only if the transferring power "has satisfied itself of the willingness and ability" of the receiving power to observe the requirements of the Convention. If, after transfer, the receiving power does not do so, then the original captor power must "take effective steps to correct the situation or shall request the return of the prisoners." Under the Geneva Protection of Civilians Convention, the same provisions apply to civilian prisoners.

In view of the South Vietnamese record of prisoner mistreatment, it might well be doubted whether the circumstances of transfer of our prisoners to their hands was in compliance with these requirements. It is true that in 1966 the American commander-in-chief in Vietnam categorically declared that the transferred prisoners were being treated in accordance with the Convention.[17]

Confidence in the accuracy of this statement was badly shaken in the summer of 1970, as the result of a visit to Con Son prison by two Congressmen who were in South Vietnam as members of a special committee of the House of Representatives. Atrocious conditions, including the use of windowless pits called "tiger cages," were reported by the Congressmen, but it was not made clear whether any of the prisoners had previously been in American custody. However, a simultaneous report from an American Friends Service doctor, who had observed evidences of extensive torture of the inmates of a South Vietnamese interrogation center in Quang Ngai (the capital of the province in which Son My is situated), was even more disturbing, as it indicated that some of the victims had been sent there by the Americans, and that an American "intelligence adviser" was attached to the center and familiar with the circumstances.[18]

Whatever problems of treaty interpretation may complicate the issue of American responsibility for South Vietnamese treatment of prisoners are wholly lacking in connection with the criminal implications of the trial of Lieutenant Duffy, charged before an Army court-martial in Long Binh with the murder of an unarmed Vietnamese civilian prisoner in September, 1969. The gist of the charge was that Duffy had ordered or allowed one of his sergeants to shoot the prisoner, who had been found hiding in a "hootch," and kept tied to a stake during the night before the shooting was done.

Duffy's defense was that according to his understanding of Army policy, the "body count" was the measure of military success, and that in killing the Vietnamese prisoner he was simply following that policy. In support of this defense, four other lieutenants from the same battalion testified that their instructions were to take no prisoners in combat, and that their superiors laid primary stress on the body count.

This was strong medicine indeed. In the heat of battle, killing enemy soldiers seeking to surrender is not unusual, as we have seen. But a policy of refusing to take prisoners—a denial of quarter, in the old phrase—has long been condemned by the customary laws of war, as it is in The Hague Convention of 1907 and in the military regulations of all modern armies. Furthermore, the Duffy case was not a combat killing, as the prisoner was unarmed and safely secured.

In response to the testimony of the four lieutenants, the Pentagon at once denied that Army practice tolerated killing prisoners, and labeled such conduct as "murder." But the military court hearing the case, after convicting Duffy of murder, revoked the verdict, convicted him of involuntary manslaughter, and sentenced him to six months' confinement. No reasons for the decision were given, but the change of front, coupled with the undisputed testimony of the four lieutenants, strongly suggests that the judges found some substance in the defense.[19]

Such are some of the more disturbing features of our operations in Vietnam, and such is the setting of the Son My killings, which threw the spotlight of publicity into these dark corners: forced resettlement of millions of rural families with utterly inadequate provision for their health and human dignity; complicity in the torture of prisoners by our wards, the South Vietnamese; enthusiasm for body counts overriding the laws of war on the taking of prisoners; devastation of large areas of the country in order to expose the insurgents; outlawry of every visible human being in the free-fire zones; slaughter of the villagers of Son My even to the infants-in-arms.

Are these things a terrible, mad aberration, or can cause and responsibility be traced? In part, no doubt, they are due to the features of the Vietnam conflict which have made the laws of war unusually difficult of application. The enemy does not respect those laws, the terrain lends itself to clandestine operations in which women and children frequently participate, the hostile and the friendly do not label themselves as such, and individuals of the yellow race are hard for our soldiers to identify. As in the Philippines 65 years ago, our troops are thousands of miles from home in uncomfortable, dangerous and unfamiliar surroundings. No one not utterly blind to the realities can fail to acknowledge and make allowance for the difficulties and uncertainties they face in distinguishing inoffensive noncombatants from hostile partisans.

These unlovely circumstances were not the creation of Lieut. James Duffy, who encouraged his sergeant to shoot the helpless prisoner, or of the company and platoon commanders who led their men into Son My, or of Marine Pvt. Michael Schwarz, sentenced to life imprisonment by a military court in Danang, for participating in the killing of 12 Vietnamese villagers.[20] Are they alone to be held accountable?

# 7 / Crime and Punishment

OPINION OR "REACTION" samplings taken shortly after th  first news of the Son My incidents
revealed that nearly two-thirds of those interviewed
denied feeling any shock. Some observers found
this lack of public indignation or shame, as well as
some of the comments recorded by the samplers,
more upsetting than the killings themselves.[1]

It is neither surprising nor particularly disturbing,
however, that many of those interviewed refused
to believe that anything untoward had occurred.
"I can't believe an American serviceman would
purposely shoot any civilian," declared Alabama's
George Wallace, "any atrocities in this war were
caused by the Communists." Others described the
reports as "a prefabricated story by a bunch of
losers," or labeled them incredible because "it's

contrary to everything I've learned about America."
These outright rejections of undisputed information
are a familiar defense mechanism, activated in
order to ward off the shock which would accompany acceptance.

There was also a widespread disposition to dis-
count the Son My stories on the ground that "incidents such as this are bound to happen in a war."
So, too, are murders and robberies "bound to happen" in our streets, and they are likely to happen
much more often if we cease to regard them as
reprehensible. In fact Son My was unusual, both
in its scale and the candor with which the operation
was carried on, with Army photographers on the
scene and commanders in helicopters circling over-
head. Those who resorted to this "sloughing-off"
justification are, nonetheless, correct in assuming
that unjustifiable killings of prisoners and civilians
on a smaller scale are bound to and indeed do happen in a war, and what they overlook is that in the
United States Army, when detected they have generally not gone unpunished. During the Second
World War many American soldiers were court-
martialed and severely punished for killing or as-
saulting civilians in violation of local law or the
laws of war. The fact that we are now fighting in
Asia instead of Europe is hardly a worthy basis for
suspending their application.

Nevertheless, there is one respect in which the
public reaction, insofar as those interviewed were
slow to denounce the troops who did the shooting
at Son My, is sound. The thought is rarely articulated, and yet may well be lurking in the back of

the mind, that if there is criminal guilt in this episode, it does not lie most heavily on the shoulders
of those who, at least up to now, are being brought
to trial. There may also be grounds for doubt that
Army court-martial proceedings at Fort McPherson,
Fort Benning, or some other Army post are the
most suitable forum in which to test the issues that
Son My raises. These questions, taken in reverse
order, are the substance of this chapter.

In the long wake of the Son My disclosures,
about a dozen soldiers—a company and a platoon
commander, noncoms and privates—faced criminal
charges for their parts in the incident. Defense
lawyers made motions and brought a number of
legal actions, in Army channels and in the Federal courts, to delay or prevent the court-martial
proceedings. The situation was further complicated
because a number of the soldiers involved at Son
My had been discharged from service before the
Army took official cognizance of the killings, and
there was a question whether these men might be
brought to trial at all, as the Supreme Court has
held that ex-servicemen cannot be court-martialed
for offenses committed while in service.[2]

One point that was much pressed by defense counsel and others was the extraordinary amount and in-
tensity of the publicity that followed the Son My
disclosures, and its possibly prejudicial effect on the
trial proceedings. This, of course, is a general problem in the administration of justice which has been
the subject of wide concern in recent years, and
especially since the Warren Commission's comments

on the conduct of police and press at the time of President Kennedy's assassination. Under the rubric of "fair trial and free press," the problem has stimulated a flood of books and articles, and I confess having myself contributed to the glut.[3] Bar and press associations have waged a war of words over the proper balance between the needs of justice and what the journalists call the public's "right to know." The Supreme Court underlined the gravity of the matter in 1966, by overturning the murder conviction of Dr. Samuel H. Sheppard, on the ground that his notorious trial in 1954 had been unfair "because of the trial judge's failure to protect Sheppard sufficiently from the massive, pervasive and prejudicial publicity that attended his prosecution."[4]

There is no gainsaying the seriousness of this problem in the case of the Son My defendants, for the television and newspaper publicity was indeed glaring and often accusatory. Most of it would not have been tolerated under the much more rigorous standards observed in Britain, where pretrial publicity can be and often is the basis for criminal contempt penalties against the offending news organs.

But it has never been, and should not now be, the rule that publicity furnishes the basis for not proceeding against an accused individual at all—in effect, for granting him immunity from prosecution because of the publicity that has surrounded his case. After all, Jack Ruby was tried for murder after millions of television viewers had watched him pump a bullet into Lee Oswald's stomach, and while this would have made it very difficult for

Ruby to deny that he fired the fatal shot, no one seriously suggested that he must therefore escape justice entirely. There is simply no way that sensational crimes can be kept out of the press, especially when most of the publicity precedes the apprehension or accusation of those eventually charged.

A much more doubtful question is whether an Army general court-martial is an appropriate judicial forum for the trial of the Son My cases. On the face of things the charges are simple enough—that Lieutenant X or Corporal Y killed or assaulted one or more human beings—but, as has been seen, the simplicity is deceptive, and searching issues of fact and law start from the cases at every turn.

If matters follow the customary course, the courts-martial will be "convened" by the commanding general of the post or military area within which the trial is to be held. This means that the commander will designate the members of the court, who function essentially like a jury, except that they not only determine guilt or innocence, but also fix the sentence if the defendant is found guilty. The members will be subordinates of the commander, will probably not be lawyers, and, since none of those as yet charged with responsibility for Son My is of high rank, the members of the court need not be. Presiding over the proceedings will be a military judge, responsible not to the commander but to the Army Judge Advocate General in Washington. The judge will wear a black robe, so that his rank will not be visible though everyone will know what it is, and he will instruct the court on such legal issues as may arise. The court's judgment is subject to review as of right in a Court of Military Review responsible to the Judge Advocate General, and may then be reviewed by the civilian Court of Military Appeals, if that body thinks the case important enough to warrant its attention.

Consider the issues that are likely to confront a court-martial in the Son My cases, bearing in mind that the defendants are represented by counsel, several of whom are not only able but also very prominent in legal circles. In its strictest form, as we have seen, "superior orders" as a defense depends on whether or not the defendant knew the order to be unlawful. Of course, it will first have to be determined what orders were in fact given to the troops entering Son My, but let us assume that the soldiers could reasonably have thought that they were being told or encouraged to kill the inhabitants. What did "unlawful" mean to them? According to their own accounts, two or three of the soldiers *did* regard the goings-on as unlawful and took no part. But what standard of "lawfulness" were they and the others instructed or trained to apply? What sort of indoctrination had they had not only from manuals or training sessions, but from observation of what was going on around them in Vietnam?

These questions lead to another very basic one: What, for present purposes, is an "order"? Everyone who has done military service knows that there are occasions when the rule-book does not fit the circumstances; no one is expected to follow it, and may even get into serious trouble if he does. The departure from the rules may be a matter of unspoken but accepted practice and it would, for example, be quite unnecessary for an officer to tell his men in so many words to take no prisoners if, by prior experience and the temper of the moment, the men sense that this is how things are going to be today.

*The ultimate question of "guilt" in the trials of the Son My troops is how far what they did departed from general American military practice in Vietnam as they had witnessed it.* This may not be germane to the question of legality under the Geneva Conventions or the Articles of War. But the defense of superior orders has its true base not in technicality but in equity, and is properly invoked by the low-ranking soldier in mitigation of punishment for conduct, even though unlawful, that is not too far removed from the behavior authorized or encouraged by his superiors in the force in which he serves.

Now, the searching feature of the situation is that this defense cannot be put forward or tested without, in substance, putting American military practice in Vietnam on trial. Who, other than the defendants and their counsel, is prepared to do that? One may well wonder whether either a judge advocate officer sitting as military judge, or a "jury" of officers appointed by a post commandant,* is likely to have much enthusiasm for such a proceeding, the evidentiary ramifications and politico-military implications of which are painfully obvious.

---

* A defendant who is an enlisted man is entitled to demand that enlisted men be included in the court, but the demand is rarely made in practice because the commanders are inclined to appoint discipline-minded top sergeants.

The shortcomings of court-martial procedure in cases of this type were sharply revealed in the case of Lieut. James Duffy, to which I have already alluded. For Duffy put forth, in miniature, the same sort of defense that may be expected, in gross, in the Son My courts-martial. He did not claim that his superior officer had ordered him to kill the Vietnamese prisoner. He and his supporting witnesses testified rather that their commanders laid emphasis on the desirability of a "high body count"; that one of their superiors had been "angry" on a prior occasion when prisoners were taken; that the practice had developed of not taking prisoners in order to increase the body count.

Was this defense factually credible? The court-martial gave no meaningful answer. The military judge instructed the court that the rules of land warfare applied to the war in Vietnam, and that the question was whether Duffy thought he was obeying an order "that a man of ordinary sense and understanding would know to be illegal." The court thereupon convicted Duffy of premeditated murder, but on being informed that this crime carries a mandatory life sentence, revoked the verdict and convicted him of involuntary manslaughter. The president of the court, Col. Robert W. Shelton, was reported to have made some reference to "the ramifications to the Army" of Duffy's defense. According to the account in The New York Times:

*Several military lawyers attending the court-martial as spectators said privately that a full acquittal of Lieutenant Duffy would have been damaging to the Army. The Army, they said,*

*already was under heavy pressure because of
the publicity about the alleged Son My massacre and other suspected war crimes.*

*"But the court didn't want to make Duffy
suffer that badly to get the Army off the hook,"
said one young law officer. "To a lot of us it
looks like another example of the M.G.R.—the
mere gook rule—being applied," he asserted.*

*He explained that the expression had been
adopted facetiously by some Army legal officers
who believed that military courts were lenient
to Americans who killed Vietnamese civilians,
because the Vietnamese were regarded as
somehow second-class human beings or "mere
gooks."⁵*

What is one to make of all this? "Involuntary
manslaughter" denotes an unintentional negligent
killing, and is a singularly inappropriate label for
the conduct on which Duffy's conviction was based.
To reverse the famous Gilbertian line, the crime
was made to fit the punishment.

If ever a case cried out for an explanatory opinion, it is this one, but opinions are not part of court-
martial practice. If the court had thought Duffy's
defense to be fabricated, it is hard to see why the
murder conviction was revoked, since the willful
killing of an unarmed, helpless prisoner abundantly
supports it. If there was in fact no such body count
practice as Duffy and his witnesses described, could
Duffy nevertheless have believed that it existed?
That is unlikely, and the inference seems inescap-
able that the members of the court believed the

body count testimony, at least in part, and gave it decisive effect in mitigation. But who was responsible for the body count practice, and how widespread is it?

This last is the question that no ordinary court-martial will want to answer, and one over which many in high authority may wish to draw a veil. And since it is also the question that most deeply affects the integrity of the Army, it is the one that most needs answering. An ordinary court-martial is not a body of sufficient stature or independence to grapple with such far-ranging and ominous matters. It may wish to convict so that the Army will not "look bad," and cloak its actual reasons in silence. It is too easily swayed by what Colonel Shelton called "ramifications to the Army," and unable to articulate the legal or moral significance of what it does.

Both in fairness to the defendants and in response to the public need, accordingly, there is much to be said for trying the Son My cases before a special military commission, to which able civilian judges and lawyers, outside the military chain of command, might be appointed. As has been seen, the defense of superior orders does not eliminate criminal responsibility but rather shifts it upward, and that is the direction in which an ordinary court-martial will be least anxious to look.

The Duffy case was not the first in which the defense was based on the assertion that war crimes in Vietnam are not isolated atrocities, but are a manifestation of command policy. In 1967, Dr. Howard

B. Levy, then a captain in the Army medical service, was court-martialed on charges that included disobedience to orders in that he refused to give medical training to "aidmen" of the Special Forces, better known as "Green Berets." At his trial, Levy justified his refusal on the ground that American troops in Vietnam were committing war crimes, and that he therefore should not train troops about to be sent there. Surprisingly, the military judge allowed him to offer evidence in support of his contention, but on short notice his lawyers were unable to satisfy the judge that there was a criminal "pattern of practice" in Vietnam. In any event, the argument was fraught with difficulties; nothing decided at Nuremberg or elsewhere suggests that a soldier is entitled to disobey an intrinsically legal order at Fort Jackson because other soldiers, halfway round the world, are given illegal orders. Such a theory would equally justify the cook in refusing to feed the aidmen.

But Dr. Levy had another argument, which was not sharply articulated until later—that the order to train the aidmen was itself illegal and in violation of medical ethics. According to the evidence he submitted to the court, Green Beret aidmen engaged in combat. They were "soldiers first and aidmen second." Furthermore, it was their purpose to use medicine as a political lever, and Green Beret publicity described the "use of medicine as a weapon."

Under the laws of war, doctors, nurses and medical corpsmen are military personnel, but they are noncombatants, like chaplains. They are expected to treat enemy wounded, carry special medical identity cards and are entitled to wear or display the Red Cross and be immune from deliberate enemy attack. The Geneva conventions and the Army rules of land warfare draw a clear separation between combat troops and noncombat medical personnel, and condemn misuse of medical noncombat status or of the Red Cross emblem.

Accordingly, there was at least some basis for argument that Dr. Levy was being unlawfully ordered to train the aidmen in unlawful activities. Furthermore, the dispensation of medicines by unqualified persons, or on a politically selective basis or as a bribe, raises serious questions of medical ethics as well as bare legality.

Nevertheless, Levy's contention failed, and he served a prison term at Leavenworth. The case is important for present purposes because of the military judge's ruling that evidence in support of criminal command practice was to be admitted— a ruling that was sure to be cited in support of comparable offers of proof in the Son My proceedings. It is an ironic touch that Dr. Levy submitted the evidence to justify disobedience to orders, whereas the Son My defendants would offer it to establish that they were obeying orders.*

While the Army legal services were interrogating, clearing, and charging the soldiers involved at Son

---

* In June, 1970, Daniel A. Switkes, a captain in the Army medical service, brought suit in the New York Federal court asking that the Army be enjoined from sending him to Indochina, basing his case in part on the contention that he was "entitled not to be forced to become an accomplice to war crimes."

My, the incident was under investigation by two other bodies. One of these is a special subcommittee of the House Armed Services Committee, officially entitled the "My Lai Incident Subcommittee," composed of four Congressmen and chaired by F. Edward Hébert of Louisiana. The other was an inquiry initiated by the Secretary of the Army and the Army Chief of Staff, and conducted by Lieut. Gen. William R. Peers, into the reasons why high-level review of the Son My killings had been so long delayed.

The Hébert subcommittee issued its report on July 14, 1970, in which it declared that what happened at Son My "was so wrong and so foreign to the normal character and action of our military forces as to immediately raise a question as to the legal sanity at the time of those men involved." More significant were the subcommittee's conclusions that the "My Lai matter was covered up within the Americal Division and by the district and province advisory teams," and that the Army had been most uncooperative: "The manner in which most of the Americal Division officers, in both command and staff capacities, testified before the subcommittee suggests an extreme reluctance on their part to discuss the allegation and its justification with any real specificity." An angry Chairman Hébert declared that "the committee was hampered by the Department of the Army in every conceivable way."[6]

General Peers submitted his report on March 14, 1970, but only portions of it have been made public, for the stated and apparently sufficient reason that release of the restricted parts might "prejudice the rights of defendants in current and potential criminal proceedings."[7] He concluded "that there were serious deficiencies in the actions taken by officials in the Americal Division, the 11th Brigade, and Task Force Barker, after the incident at Son My," in that those officials did not "take appropriate action to investigate or report." On this basis he recommended that charges of "dereliction of duty and failure to obey regulations," and in some cases of "false swearing," be brought against 14 officers, ranging in rank from captain to major general.

The matter was then transferred to the jurisdiction of Lieut. Gen. Mathew O. Seaman, commander of the First Army at Fort Meade in Maryland, who shortly announced dismissal, for lack of evidence, of the charges against seven of the officers.[*] The seven remaining under charges included the commanders, at the time of Son My, of the Americal Division and the 11th Brigade, to which Task Force Barker was subordinated.

Why was the Son My incident "covered up" by the Army? The published portions of the Peers report do not reach that question. What has been released is, however, of great interest in that it describes the history and training of the units and headquarters involved at Son My, and mentions and quotes from a number of the tactical and other directives that are supposed to govern the conduct of military operations in Vietnam.

---

[*] One of the officers cleared by General Seaman had invoked the privilege against self-incrimination while testifying before the Hébert subcommittee.

On their face, as regards the laws of war, the directives are virtually impeccable. United States forces observe the Geneva conventions, and all military personnel are to be adequately indoctrinated in their provisions. All troops arriving in Vietnam are to receive "information cards," covering treatment of "The Enemy in Your Hands," and stressing "humanitarian treatment and respect for the Vietnamese people." The "Rules of Engagement" issued by the American commander in Vietnam, then Gen. William Westmoreland, instructed the troops to "use your fire power with care and discrimination, particularly in populated areas." Another directive stipulated that fire power should be so used as to avoid "incidents involving friendly forces, noncombatants, and damage to civilian property." Directly pertinent to Son My was the directive on minimization of civilian casualties, which called for protection of the inhabitant "whether at any one time he lives in a VC or GVN [Government of Vietnam] controlled hamlet," since whether it is the one or the other may well depend "to a large extent upon factors and forces beyond his control." The instructions issued by the headquarters of the 11th Brigade were generally in line with these directives.

But of course the question remains whether the picture painted by these directives bears any resemblance to the face of war in Vietnam, and on this score, once again, the Peers report as published is silent. Of what use is an hour or two of lectures on the Geneva Conventions if the soldier sent into combat sees them flouted on every side? How does the admonition to the Air Force square with the observations of Jonathan Schell on the way in which tactical air power is actually used, or with the Marine "ultimatum" that he quotes? How "real" do the instructions to the ground troops appear in the light of the lieutenants' testimony at the Duffy trial, of the "mere gook" rule described by the Army lawyers, or of the Army major's remark after the destruction of Ben Tre, with heavy loss of civilian life: "It was necessary to destroy the town to save it"?[8]

Despite the careful wording of the orders and the optimistic releases from the Pentagon about "pacification," virtually all observers report death, destruction and troop attitudes that indicate that the restraint called for by the orders is not exercised. Shortly after the Son My disclosures, four sergeants in Vietnam wrote a letter expressing hearty approval:[9] "You know this is a VC village, they are the enemy, they are a part of the enemy's war apparatus. Our job is to destroy the enemy, so kill them . . . I want to come home alive, if I must kill old men, women or children to make myself a little safer, I'll do it without hesitation." One may indeed sympathize with the desire to "come home alive," but if that aim now requires the slaughter of all the Vietnamese who might be sympathetic to the Vietcong, then all our talk of "pacification," to say nothing of the Hague Conventions, is the sheerest hypocrisy, and we had better acknowledge at once that we are prepared to do what we hanged and imprisoned Japanese and German generals for doing.

The letter of the four sergeants, of course, does not embody Army policy, but it is indicative of

troop attitudes that the Army has allowed to develop and, alas, in many cases to prevail. The attitudes themselves are a natural product of the surroundings and nature of the war. The Vietcong do
infiltrate and dominate the villages, and depend
on the rural population for both support and con-
cealment, and many of the villagers cooperate with
them, whether out of fear or favor. After a few air
strikes and "zippo raids" the villagers have less reason than before to like Americans, and so distrust
soon turns to hate, as Richard Hammer has so com-
pellingly explained:

> *Pretty soon you get to hate all these people.
> You get to fear them, too. They're all out for
> your ass one way or another, out to take you
> for everything you've got. You don't know
> which ones are your enemies and which ones
> are your friends. So you begin to think that
> they're all your enemies. And that all of them
> are something not quite human, some kind of
> lower order of creature. You give them names
> to depersonalize them, to categorize them as
> you've become convinced they ought to be
> categorized. They become dinks and slopes
> and slants and gooks, and you begin to say,
> and believe, "The only good dink is a dead
> dink." You echo the comments of your buddies
> that, "One million of them ain't worth one of
> us. We should blow up all those slant-eyed
> bastards."[10]*

Other witnesses tell much the same story: retired
Marine Colonels James A. Donovan and William

R. Corson; Dr. Robert Jay Lifton of Yale; Dr. Gordon Livingston, a graduate of West Point and Johns Hopkins who served as a major in Vietnam. "No one has any feelings for the Vietnamese," a Texas private told Jonathan Schell. "The trouble is no one sees the Vietnamese as people. They're not people. Therefore it doesn't matter what you do to them." These attitudes are often aggravated by atrocious conduct of the Vietcong; Son My pales into numerical insignificance beside the massacre of thousands in Hue during the Tet offensive, when the Vietcong also overran Quang Ngai and raced through the hospital shooting doctors, nurses and bed-ridden patients. "One tends not to want to be too compassionate in dealing with an enemy like that," a soldier told William Beecher of The New York Times.[11]

If these observers are not to be trusted, there remains the record of what has happened. Perhaps the Department of Defense has accurate totals of South Vietnamese civilians killed, maimed and made homeless by the war, but probably much of this misery has remained untabulated and is known only to the victims. Early in 1968, the late Senator Robert Kennedy stated that our population transfers, village destruction, and defoliation had created two million refugees, in a country of sixteen million people. A year later Professor Gabriel Kolko of Buffalo put the figure at 3,153,000, apparently based on evidence given in hearings conducted by the Senate Judiciary Committee.[12] The American Friends Service Committee estimates that some 150,000 civilians have been killed *annually* by combat operations. The Saigon Government reported 26,000 civilians killed and 74,000 wounded during 1967 in the regions it controlled. To be sure, some of these were killed by the Vietcong, but the disparity of fire power as between the two sides, and American monopoly in the air, make it a certainty that we are responsible for the greater part of the civilian casualties.[13]

Whether these figures are double or half the actuality is not of much legal or moral significance. As Colonel Donovan reminds us,[14] those "who talk about the massacre of South Vietnamese that may happen at some future date if our troops leave the battlefield are apparently oblivious to the fact that a massacre of the Vietnamese people has been going on for five years, and much of the bloodshed has resulted from U.S. fire power."

The Army leadership can hardly have been blind to the probable consequences to civilians of a massive employment of American troops in Vietnam to engage in counterinsurgent operations. Indeed, General Peers called attention in his report to the dangers to noncombatants from "frequent employment of massive fire power" and from "the intermingling of the nonuniformed foe and the populace," and declared that: "Early in the conflict, these factors and many others associated with this unique war caused great concern at the highest levels for the protection of noncombatants and the minimization of casualties to those persons not directly involved." But how did this concern manifest itself, other than in the bland language of the various directives and "rules of engagement"?

We may pass until later the question whether heavy fire power should have been used at all. Assuming that decision to have been made, there is no gainsaying the difficulties that the American command faced in achieving a "minimization" of civilian casualties and maintaining a humane and considerate attitude, among the troops. "There are no agreed 'rules of land warfare' between antagonists . . . when one . . . is a regular force . . . and the other includes old men, women, and children, as well as guerrilla troops," writes Col. William Corson. "And it is doubtful such rules can even be written. However, lacking such rules, if the United States is to avoid the moral and legal dilemmas associated with brutality in warfare, not only the U.S. fighting man, but the entire American society must have a thorough knowledge of the end the United States has in view . . ."[15]

Neither the "fighting man" nor "American society" has had any such understanding, and what is far worse, neither has our political and military leadership, for such an understanding would have revealed the unsuitability of zippo raids and free-fire zones as measures to "pacify" the countryside. Still, assuming that fire power is envisaged as playing a major role in the counterinsurgency warfare, then it is plain that certain accompanying measures are urgently required to "minimize" the inevitably destructive consequences.

Before embarking on a counterinsurgency war in Indochina, for example, some of the staff planners might well have cast a glance across the South China Sea to the Philippines, where we fought a counterinsurgency campaign 70 years ago.

> Damn, damn, damn the Filipinos,
> Civilize them with a Krag

sang the soldiers in 1900, as they hunted Emilio Aguinaldo's irregulars, and today's soldier songs in Vietnam, as reported by Jonathan Schell, are redolent of the same sort of "humor."* When east and west meet in such unpleasant circumstances, racial slurs and scorns are inevitable, and probably "slope" and "dink" would have become standard Army vocabulary under the best of conditions.

Given the circumstances and purposes of the war, however, it should have been a matter of the highest priority to insure, by indoctrination and subsequent policing, that the troops should treat the Vietnamese as human beings with lives worth preserving. Unfortunately, feelings of racial superiority are not confined to enlisted men, and it is highly probable that many officers have a "mere gook rule" in the back of their minds when they order an air strike or mark out a free-fire zone. In any event, it is all too clear that the Army's attitude and performance in this area have been woefully inadequate.

American military and economic missions had been in Indochina since the end of the Second World War, and by the time President Johnson took office there were already some 15,000 military personnel in South Vietnam. It is difficult, therefore,

---

* The "Filipino" song was sung to the Civil War tune "Tramp, Tramp, Tramp, the Boys are Marching." The Krag Jorgensen rifle was the standard infantry weapon at the turn of the century. One of the Schell-reported lyrics:

> Bomb the schools and churches,
> Bomb the rice fields, too,
> Show the children in the courtyards
> What napalm can do.

to attribute the blunders that accompanied the massive build-up to lack of information. We knew the size, density of population and terrain of the country, and it must have been apparent that however good the aim and intention, the bullets, bombs and shells were going to hit a lot of buildings and people that were simply unfortunate enough to be there. Once the population transfers and search-and-destroy missions became standard practice, the prospect of heavy civilian casualties, and masses of refugees, became a certainty. Bad enough that was, but far worse the failure to provide sufficient housing and hospitals to relieve the suffering we caused, and soon the point was reached where large operations were designed so as not to "generate" refugees for lack of a place to put them.

I have stressed, and I believe rightly, the maddening difficulties and dangers that troops and commanders alike—soldiers at all levels—faced in the conditions, some of our own making, that have developed in South Vietnam as our commitment deepened. For the lower ranks, these circumstances must count powerfully in mitigation of their culpability. But in these confused, complex, and shifting circumstances, the responsibility of the higher officers for training, doctrine and practice is all the greater.

During the Second World War, the German Army in occupied Europe faced conditions that, in some countries, were not totally dissimilar to those prevailing in Vietnam, and had a like mission of "pacification." There, too, villages were destroyed and the inhabitants killed, and after the war a number of field marshals and generals implicated in the actions were brought to trial at Nuremberg in the so-called "High Command case." In summing up at the close of the trial, the prosecution dealt with this same issue of comparative responsibility as between the troops and their leaders:

*Somewhere, there is unmitigated responsibility for these atrocities. Is it to be borne by the troops? Is it to be borne primarily by the hundreds of subordinates who played a minor role in this pattern of crime? We think it is clear that that is not where the deepest responsibility lies. Men in the mass, particularly when organized and disciplined in armies, must be expected to yield to prestige, authority, the power of example, and soldiers are bound to be powerfully influenced by the examples set by their commanders. That is why . . . the only way in which the behavior of the German troops in the recent war can be made comprehensible as the behavior of human beings is by a full exposure of the criminal doctrines and orders which were pressed on them from above by these defendants and others. Who could the German Army look to, other than von Leeb and the senior field marshals, to safeguard its standards of conduct and prevent their disintegration? If a decision is to be rendered here which may perhaps help to prevent the repetition of such events, it is important above all else that responsibility be fixed where it truly belongs. Mitigation should be reserved for those upon whom superior orders are pressed down, and who lack the means to influence general standards of behavior. It is not, we submit, available to the commander who participates in bringing the criminal pressures to bear, and whose responsibility it is to insure the preservation of honorable military traditions.*[16]

When General Peers submitted his report charging several high-ranking officers with dereliction of duty in covering up Son My, the press reported sharp controversy in military circles on whether the airing of dirty linen would be "good" or "bad" for the Army as an institution. Of course, both Son My and the cover-up were indicative of serious weaknesses, but once Son My had happened, its exposure was not merely "good" but essential to the integrity of the Army's leadership. What officer with any respect or sense for the values of the military profession could serve with pride in an organization where serious crime in the lower ranks is buried in the files on orders from above? The burying is itself an offense, known to the law as "misprision of felony," and Son My could not have been permanently covered up without infecting the higher reaches of the Army leadership with criminality.

The trouble now is that the uncovering is not being carried nearly far enough. General Peers was directed to investigate only what happened *after* Son My—specifically "the adequacy of . . . investigations or inquiries and subsequent reviews and reports within the chain of command," and "whether any suppression or withholding of information by persons involved in the incident had taken place."

But so far as is publicly known, *the Army has undertaken no general investigation of the killings themselves, to determine the level of responsibility for the conditions that gave rise to Son My or the many similar though smaller incidents.*

Now the Son My court-martial proceedings carry the prospect of inquiry into those ominous problems —into body counts, and zippo raids, and free-fire zones, and "mere gook rules." The motive force will be the defendants' effort to shake off culpability either by showing that what they did was not "wrong," however unlawful, or that if wrong, others more highly placed were primarily responsible. Such an inquiry is unlikely to be either complete or dispassionate.

"Regardless of the outcome of . . . the My Lai courts-martial and other legal actions," Col. William Corson has written, "the point remains that American judgment as to the effective prosecution of the war was faulty from beginning to end and that the atrocities, alleged or otherwise, are a result of a failure of judgment, not criminal behavior." Colonel Corson overlooks, I fear, that negligent homicide is generally a crime of bad judgment rather than evil intent. Perhaps he is right in the strictly causal sense that if there had been no failure of judgment, the occasion for criminal conduct would not have arisen. The Germans in occupied Europe made gross errors of judgment which no doubt created the conditions in which the slaughter of the inhabitants of Klissura occurred, but that did not make the killings any the less criminal.

Still, there is a real question how far the criminal process is appropriate as a scale in which to weigh the responsibility of those in high authority for the crimes committed in Vietnam. The pages of The Washington Monthly and the New York Village Voice have recently been the vehicle for a running debate on the subject between Townsend Hoopes, former Under Secretary of the Air Force and author of an interesting account of top-level policy formulation from 1965 to 1969, and two newspaper reporters, Geoffrey Cowan and Judith Coburn.[17] The reporters thought that if Justice Jackson's promises at Nuremberg were to be kept, President Johnson and his associates ought to be brought before a like bar of justice; Mr. Hoopes's reaction to this, not unnaturally, was one of dismay. The antagonists never squarely locked horns, so that not even the most dispassionate judge could award the laurels of victory to either side. Mr. Hoopes's defense, nonetheless, was something less than satisfying, for the burden of it was that American leaders are intrinsically "good" men. "Lyndon Johnson, though disturbingly volatile, was not in his worst moments an evil man in the Hitlerian sense," Mr. Hoopes declared, while "his principal advisers were, almost uniformly, those considered to be among the ablest, the best, the most humane and liberal men that could be found for public trust."

That is what trial lawyers call "character testimony." Whatever its value in a fraud or perjury case, it is not very relevant to a determination whether certain proven conduct is criminal, and whether the defendant was implicated. How much the President and his close advisers in the White

House, Pentagon and Foggy Bottom knew about the volume and cause of civilian casualties in Vietnam, and the physical devastation of the countryside, is speculative. Something was known, for the late John McNaughton (then Assistant Secretary of Defense) returned from the White House one day in 1967 with the message that "We seem to be proceeding on the assumption that the way to eradicate the Vietcong is to destroy all the village structures, defoliate all the jungles, and then cover the entire surface of South Vietnam with asphalt."[18]

Whatever the limits and standards of culpability for civilians in Washington, the proximity and immediate authority of the military commanders ties the burden of responsibility much more tightly to their shoulders. The divisional and other commands in Quang Ngai Province, within which Son My is situated and where civilian casualties and physical destruction have been especially heavy, were subordinated to the Third Marine Amphibious Force, commanded by Lieut. Gen. Robert E. Cushman, who in turn was directly responsible to the top Army headquarters in Vietnam, the Military Assistance Command Vietnam (MACV). At the time of Son My, Gen. William Westmoreland headed MACV, with Gen. Creighton Abrams as his deputy, and Lieut. Gen. William B. Rossen in charge of a headquarters of MACV in northern South Vietnam. From MACV, the chain of command runs through the Commander-in-Chief Pacific (Adm. Ulysses Grant Sharp Jr.) to the Chiefs of Staff in Washington.

It is on these officers that command responsibility for the conduct of operations has lain. From General Westmoreland down they were more or less constantly in Vietnam, and splendidly equipped with helicopters and other aircraft, which gave them a degree of mobility unprecedented in earlier wars, and consequently endowed them with every opportunity to keep the course of the fighting and its consequences under close and constant observation. Communications were generally rapid and efficient, so that the flow of information and orders was unimpeded.

These circumstances are in sharp contrast to those that confronted General Yamashita in 1944 and 1945, with his forces reeling back in disarray before the oncoming American military powerhouse. For failure to control his troops so as to prevent the atrocities they committed, Brig. Gens. Egbert F. Bullene and Morris Handwerk and Maj. Gens. James A. Lester, Leo Donovan and Russel B. Reynolds found him guilty of violating the laws of war and sentenced him to death by hanging. The sentence was first confirmed by the area commander, Lieut. Gen. William D. Styer, and then by Gen. Douglas MacArthur, as Commander-in-Chief, United States Army Forces in the Pacific. In his statement on the confirmation, General MacArthur said of Yamashita:

> It is not easy for me to pass penal judgment upon a defeated adversary in a major military campaign. I have reviewed the proceedings in vain search for some mitigating circumstance on his behalf. I can find none. Rarely has so cruel and wanton a record been spread to pub-

*lic gaze. Revolting as this may be in itself, it pales before the sinister and far-reaching implication thereby attached to the profession of arms. . . . This officer, of proven field merit, entrusted with high command involving authority adequate to responsibility, has failed this irrevocable standard; has failed his duty to his troops, to his country, to his enemy, to mankind; has failed utterly his soldier faith. The transgressions resulting therefrom as revealed by the trial are a blot upon the military profession, a stain upon civilization and constitute a memory of shame and dishonor that can never be forgotten . . .*

*I approve the findings and sentence of the Commission and direct the Commanding General, Army Forces in the Western Pacific, to execute the judgment upon the defendant, stripped of uniform, decorations and other appurtenances signifying membership in the military profession.*

Whether or not individuals are held to criminal account is perhaps not the most important question posed by the Vietnam war today. But the Son My courts-martial are shaping the question for us, and they can not be fairly determined without full inquiry into the higher responsibilities. Little as the leaders of the Army seem to realize it, this is the only road to the Army's salvation, for its moral health will not be recovered until its leaders are willing to scrutinize their behavior by the same standards that their revered predecessors applied to Tomayuki Yamashita 25 years ago.

# 8 / War and Peace

"WHY WE ARE IN VIETNAM is today a question of mainly historical interest. We *are* there, for better or for worse, and we must deal with the situation that exists." So read the opening words of Arthur M. Schlesinger Jr.'s 1967 study of American involvement in Vietnam.[1] But the reasons why we are in Vietnam are part of "the situation that exists," and the question—what those reasons are—is both a moral and a practical issue of great moment.

Consider the conflicting versions of our Vietnam purposes even within the White House circle. Early in 1967 Walt W. Rostow, then a close adviser to President Johnson, told a meeting of college student editors that our "intervention had been based legally on obligations under SEATO to resist aggression." His statement was immediately and publicly challenged by Richard N. Goodwin, a former assistant to Presidents Kennedy and Johnson, who declared that the United States had not acted under treaty obligations, but rather "because, in the judgment of the Presidents, American power and interests demanded it."

The same contrast is manifest in the explanations of United States policy given by Eugene V. Rostow, Walt's brother and former Under Secretary of State, in the course of a long interview with William Whitworth of *The New Yorker*.[2] Speaking of American policy in India and South Vietnam, Rostow declared that "our interest is not to protect democracy as such but to deter, prevent, or defeat aggression." Then at another point he described the motivation of our intervention in Vietnam as based on the Government's being concerned about "the long-range impact a withdrawal would have on Japanese policy," and being "afraid that the enormous masses and the geographical and strategic areas of that region will fall into the hands of hostile or potentially hostile powers."

In an earlier chapter, I have stated my opinion that the courts cannot reasonably be expected to pass judgment on the legality of our Vietnam policies. But to say that the judges should not answer the question is not to deny the reality and significance of the question itself. Dean Rusk had no warrant of authority to determine for all men and all time that North Vietnam committed aggression against South Vietnam. It may be unlikely that our leaders will be called upon to answer at the bar of some future international tribunal, but there is also the bar of history. As a nation dedicated to liberty, justice and peace on earth it is surely incumbent on us to engage in hard self-scrutiny, and conform our actions, as far as humanly possible, to the principles we profess.

Are we, then, acting in Vietnam as a global policeman, under the Nuremberg principles and the United Nations Charter, to "deter, prevent or defeat aggression"? Or are we promoting "American power and interests" in Asia? Enormously different consequences would flow from the dominance of one or the other of these purposes—differences in the suitability of particular military tactics, in the weight to be given to the attitude of other nations toward our actions, and in the terms of an acceptable armistice or peace settlement.

If preservation of the American position in Southeast Asia is the governing motive, then the question whether North or South Vietnam "struck the first blow" is of only collateral significance; whichever was the more to blame, America would be equally disadvantaged by a victory for the North. Essentially, we would be back to 19th century notions of legitimacy, when Lieber could describe war as an "acknowledged . . . means to obtain great ends of state." Perhaps that is still our international ethic. The Bay of Pigs was an unsuccessful but hardly a defensive operation; it was our counterpart to the Anglo-French fiasco at Suez. Nevertheless, one may suspect that in both cases the failure was largely due to the attacker's feelings of guilt, which inhibited us, as it did the British and French, from striking hard enough to achieve a prompt *fait accompli.*

Some of our other military ventures, especially in this hemisphere, have been less than simon-pure in terms of Nuremberg principles. Nevertheless, there is a deeply idealistic strain in the American interventionist tradition. In 1898, President McKinley justified the war against Spain: "In the cause of humanity and to put an end to the barbarities, bloodshed, starvation, and horrible miseries now existing" in Cuba. Thereafter, the United States joined with other governments in denouncing the Rumanian and Russian pogroms, especially at Kishinev, and the Turkish massacres of Armenians in 1915.

The idea that a government's treatment of its own nationals can be so contrary to civilized standards as to constitute an international crime, indeed, lies at the root of the "crimes against humanity" concept of the London Charter, and of the Genocide Convention.[3] And it was in this spirit that President Eisenhower pledged support to South Vietnam in 1954, telling President Ngo Dinh Diem that it was our purpose to "discourage any who might wish to impose a foreign ideology on your free people." In fact, the people were certainly not as "free" as the President thought; nevertheless, as Arthur Schlesinger puts it, the mood in which the Government started into Vietnam was "essentially moralistic."

To be sure, idealistic and selfish motives are not mutually exclusive, and sometimes work in conjunction. The North Korean attack against South Korea in 1950 was a far greater threat to Japan and the General American position in Asia than ever was Ho Chi Minh, and very likely the United States

would have intervened whatever the Korean rights
and wrongs might have been. In fact it was a clear
case of aggression by North Korea, and the United
Nations soon put its stamp of approval on the
American action, which thus became a multilateral
operation under an umbrella of international consensus.

I have already indicated my belief that one of
the difficulties about applying the Nuremberg
"crimes against peace" standards to our Vietnam
venture is the diversity of impressions and motives
that governed the many men who have influenced
the course of the operation over the 16 years that
it has now been under way. Things may not have
looked the same to President Johnson in 1964 as
they had to Eisenhower 10 years earlier; if, as has
been reported, Johnson was strongly moved by a
desire not to be "the first American President to lose
a war,"[4] one can only say that this was hardly a
worthy reaction to a problem of the greatest moment to the nation, and would not be a strong defense in any forum.

Lacking the documents and testimony to establish the personal intentions of the movers and shak-
ers in Washington, we are thrown back to the record
of what the United States Government has actually
*done* in Vietnam. On that record, it is difficult not to
reach a harsh verdict. If the primary purpose had
remained, as Eisenhower said, to protect South
Vietnam from the imposition of a "foreign ideology" or, as the Rostow brothers tell us, to deter
aggression, it is inconceivable that our conduct of
military operations should have taken the course

187

that it has. Whatever peace-keeping and protective intentions may have governed our initial involvement in Vietnam have by now been so completely submerged under the avalanche of death and destruction that they no longer are credible descriptions of the operation as a whole. Colonel Corson has summed up the consequences in a mordant pun: The United States in Vietnam has become an "international lethal aid society."

Why did things go so wrong? Some say it is because our leaders were war criminals. Whether or not that be so, it is an unsatisfactory answer in terms of causation, for it assumes that the leaders wanted things to turn out as they have, whereas in fact it is plain that those responsible are exceedingly dissatisfied with the present consequences of their policies. Surely Lyndon Johnson would never have done what he did in 1964 and 1965 if he could have foreseen the results in 1968.

I think that Colonel Corson is much closer to the truth—or truths—in saying that "American judgment as to the effective prosecution of the war was faulty from beginning to end"; that we became "over-involved militarily in the armed forces of the present, under-involved politically in the human forces of the future"; and that in the upshot our political and military leaders alike lost sight of the old law of war that "it is a mistake, illegal and immoral, to kill people without clear military advantage in a war."

That is more enlightening on the "how" than the "why" we got off course. On the second question the record is still incomplete and cloudy, but the accounts and comments of those on the edge of the inner circle strongly indicate that there was a misfit between ends and means; that the military leaders never grasped the essentially political aims of intervention, and the political leaders neglected or were unable to police the means that the military adopted to fulfill what they conceived to be their mission.

If the objective of our Vietnam policy be stated over-simply as "to stop Communism at the 17th parallel," there were at most two ways to do that. The first, which has been our stated policy, is to gain and hold the political allegiance of the South Vietnamese to a non-Communist government, while giving them defensive assistance against any military means used by the North. The second was to ignore the South Vietnamese people, treat South Vietnam as a battlefield, and kill all the North Vietnamese or Vietcong found on or moving toward the battlefield. The sad story of America's venture in Vietnam is that the military means rapidly submerged the political ends, and the first method soon gave way to the second.

Whether or not the first method could have been successfully employed is and will remain an unanswered question. After the Second World War it worked well for us in Greece, but Vietnam is quite another place. After Ho Chi Minh's long and eventually successful struggle against the French, it is at least doubtful that any Western power—perhaps any outside power—could effectively participate in Vietnam's internecine troubles. The

United States had few scholars or diplomats expert in Vietnamese institutions. Still, there were those who thought in these terms, including Roger Hilsman and Walt Rostow(!) who in 1962 "developed a cogent and comprehensive 'strategic concept for counterinsurgency' that emphasized . . . subordination of military actions to political purpose, and reliance on small scale counter guerrilla units, as opposed to conventional military formations."[5]

According to Townsend Hoopes, the Army was strongly opposed to these projects, and it is easy to see why: The regular armed services have no capacity for such undertakings. That being so, it was a possible conclusion that Vietnam was a good place for the Army to stay out of, and that was precisely the conclusion reached in 1954 by the Chief of Army Plans, Lieut. Gen. James M. Gavin. It was his opinion that "as a military operation Vietnam made no sense," because "unless the people of the country prefer the government supported by foreign troops to the guerrillas, the mere introduction of large numbers of ground troops with modern equipment would not resolve the military conflict."[6]

But what the Army and Air Force had, in great abundance, was mobility and firepower, and what they thought would be adequate manpower. Confronted with what appeared to be a deteriorating situation in South Vietnam, President Johnson and his advisers clutched for the means at hand without sufficiently considering their suitability for the end in view.

The bankruptcy of the firepower tactic did not go unobserved. "My feeling is that you could kill every Vietcong and North Vietnamese in South Vietnam and still lose the war," said the commandant of the Marine Corps, Gen. Wallace M. Greene. "Unless we can make a success of the civic-action program, we are not going to achieve the objectives we have set."[7] But neither Pentagon nor White House gave heed. Townsend Hoopes remained uncertain whether President Johnson "never understood the incompatibility of Westmoreland's ground strategy with his own stated political objective, i.e. to gain the political allegiance of the people of South Vietnam," or whether "he regarded the political aim as mere words and the need for military victory as the only governing reality."

However that may be, neither the President nor the Secretary of Defense, Robert McNamara, gave effective review to Westmoreland's operations. "The preferred military doctrine dictated the strategy, and the strategy determined the policy," says Hoopes, adding that "during nearly three years of steadily rising combat and casualty levels, Washington did not seriously question or modify the Westmoreland strategy of attrition." The Pentagon simply lost sight of "the truth that protection for the people against Vietcong terror had to be achieved by means that did not themselves alienate the people by causing heavy civilian casualties and wanton physical destruction."[8]

By the summer of 1968, it had become painfully apparent that the Westmoreland firepower tactic, apart from the moral and legal aspects, was a mili-

tary failure. Heavy casualties had been inflicted
on the Vietcong, but they remained undefeated.
"There is considerable evidence," writes Gen. David
Shoup, retired commandant of the Marine Corps,
"that the National Liberation Front is in fact better
organized and enjoys greater loyalty among the
people of Vietnam than does the Saigon government."[9]

In this costly miscalculation, the Pentagon leaders were not only deaf to the warnings of General
Gavin and others, but also blind to the lessons of
recent military history. After the Second World
War, the Army embarked on an intensive study of
the German military record, presumably to see
what lessons could be learned. The lessons were
there, to be sure, but their meaning does not seem
to have fastened itself in the American military
mind.

Consider once again the massacre of Greek villagers at Klissura, described in an earlier chapter.[10]
When this incident became known to the German
civilian authorities in Greece, whose principal interest was in pacification of the occupied country,
there was prompt and fiery protest to the German
commander-in-chief, Field Marshal Maximilian von
Weichs. The message came from Hermann Neubacher, the Foreign Office Plenipotentiary in Southeast Europe:

    . . . *It is utter insanity to murder babies,
children, women and old men because heavily
armed Red bandits billeted themselves over-
night, by force, in their houses, and because
they killed two German soldiers near the vil-*

*lage. The political effect of this senseless blood
bath doubtlessly by far exceeds the effect of all
propaganda efforts in our fight against communism.*

*No matter what the final result of the investi-
gation may be, the operation against Klissura
represents a severe transgression of existing
orders. The wonderful result of this heroic deed
is that babies are dead. But the partisans continue to live and they will again find quarters
by use of submachine guns in completely de-
fenseless villages. It is a further fact that it is
much more comfortable to shoot to death entirely harmless women, children, and old men
than to pursue an armed band with a manly
desire for vengeance and to kill them to the
last man. The use of such methods must necessarily lead to the demoralization of genuine
combat morale.*[11]

Ambassador Neubacher was not alone in his per-
ception of the self-defeating nature of such measures. In July, 1943, the Austrian General Edmund
von Glaise-Horstenau admonished the German Air
Force commanders in the Balkans that their reprisal
bombing raids on villages "forces additional people
into the woods and shakes confidence in the German soldier of those parts of the population that
are friendly to us." From Serbia, a German Army
captain reported on the harmful effects of shooting
innocent persons:

> *. . . Above all, the psychological effect will
> be catastrophic. The residents of Kragujevac
> had hoped that the German Wehrmacht would*

*rid them of the Communist danger and that
they would be aligned into the new framework
of Europe. With the methods applied here we
shall most certainly fail to win back the favor-
ably inclined elements of the population. . . .*[12]

Perhaps the most forceful denunciation of German "search-and-destroy" tactics came from a German civilian official in Belgrade a few months after
the occupation of Yugoslavia began, when a German Army captain was killed by a "Communist"
who "had been lying in ambush in the cornfield
and fled through the corn to the woods after committing the deed." In reprisal the Germans shot a
number of nearby farmers, and then took more extensive measures, as described in the official's protest to the German commander in Serbia:

> . . . *In order to combat Communist opera-
> tions which had got out of hand during the last
> few days, the German headquarters sent a
> motorized assault troop which is at present
> going through all the villages making arrests
> and, due to ignorance of the situation, is kill-
> ing innocent men, women, and children. . . .*
> *The consequence of the procedure of the
> German assault troops will be that a large num-
> ber of innocent people will be slaughtered and
> that the Communists in the woods not only
> will not be exterminated but will increase in
> numbers. Because many farmers, even entire
> villages—even though up to now they had
> no connection with the Communists—will flee
> into the woods only out of fear and will be re-*

*ceived there by the Communists. They will be*
*provided with arms and used for combat and*
*for open revolt against the German armed*
*forces. This insurrection will develop on a large*
*scale and will have incalculable and terrible*
*consequences for the entire population . . .*[18]

Now comparable reports are beginning to emerge
from Vietnam. Reprisal bombing attacks on villages have driven thousands of the inhabitants to
refugee camps, and subjected those who stay to a
fear-ridden existence. A report on refugees, done
in 1968 for the Rand Corporation, reveals that "ex-
cessive misdirected bombing" had made them hostile to the Saigon Government, and served only to
"knock the underpinnings from efforts to gain the
support of the people."[14] Two years later, as American soldiers moved into Cambodia, news correspon-
dents reported that "the pattern of Vietnam is
being repeated"; that the troops were under orders
to "burn everything," and that heavy bombing was
driving the inhabitants into the ranks of the Vietcong.[15]

And so in August, 1970, when newspaper headlines informed us "Americans in Vietnam Find
Themselves Hated," it should have come as no surprise. "The B-52 bombing raids, the air strikes on
villages where there might have been Vietcong but
maybe not, the incidents of cruelty by United States
troops—all these things have made many Vietnamese angry and outraged," wrote Gloria Emerson.[16] "The Americans are hated now because they
have, for so long, told the Vietnamese how to win
the war. Despite such assurance, the war is a long

way from being won." Now it has come to the point that Americans in Saigon can no longer walk safely alone, and are "advised to travel in pairs."

In a recent television address on the war in Southeast Asia, President Nixon coined the phrase "pitiful, helpless giant," and hotly denied that the United States, under his leadership, would play such a part. Pitiful and helpless the nation is not, but the course of events under the last three Presidents raises painful doubts whether our conduct as a nation may not have been arrogant and blind —or at best one-eyed, seeing in only one direction, and unable to perceive the lessons of the past or the trends of the present.

If an effort be made to look beneath the orders and operations and speeches and press releases for some clues to understanding the Vietnam debacle, then one must contemplate Vietnam not in isolation but in the context of the times and the many other failures and dangers that are unsettling the United States today. Most of them, I believe, can be gathered under the expression "under-maintenance," caused by our unwillingness, despite enormous material means, to invest the time, thought and resources necessary to preserve the foundations and basic services of society. Attention is given to ever taller skyscrapers, supersonic airliners and moon landings, while we pollute the air and water and allow education, transportation, housing and health to degenerate.

Despite the billions of dollars we have spent on the Vietnam war and the incredible weight of explosives dropped on that unhappy land, our failure there is largely due to *under-maintenance*. The point is implicit in the title of Jonathan Schell's book—*"The Military Half"*—as explained in a concluding passage:

> *Many optimistic Americans, including reporters as well as military men and civilian officials, tended to set off the destruction caused by the military effort against the construction resulting from the civil-affairs effort, seeing the two results as separate but balanced "sides" of the war; and, looking at our commitment of men and materials, they were often favorably impressed with the size of the constructive effort, almost as though it were being carried out in one country while the military effort was being carried out in another. But, of course, the two programs were being carried out in the same provinces and the same villages, and the people who received the allotments of rice were the same people whose villages had been destroyed by bombs. . . . Many of the civil-affairs officials were working exhaustingly long hours and doing the best job they could with their limited time and resources, and they could not see why the people should complain and expect more than they were getting. Many military men, for their part, were loyal only to their duty—that of conducting military operations. Having efficiently carried out the "military half," they saw it as the responsibility of the Vietnamese government and of the*

*American civil-affairs advisers to carry out the
"civilian half" by taking care of the people
who had been hurt or dispossessed in the "military half." . . . But because, along with the
destruction of villages, American military operations brought death to many civilians, American civil-affairs workers, no matter how well
intentioned they might be, and no matter how
well supplied they might someday become,
could never, from the point of view of the villagers, "balance" the sufferings caused by the
military, or undo what they had done, which
was often absolute and irreversible.*[17]

The "civil half" never became "well supplied"; to
paraphrase George Orwell, some halves are larger
than others, and the "military half" has been virtually the whole. Colonel Donovan has estimated
the cost of the air war alone, to the end of 1968,
at over $7-billion for bombs dropped and aircraft
lost.[18] Over half of this sum was spent on bombing
North Vietnam from early 1965 to late 1968.* The
bombing in South Vietnam has, of course, been
the principal cause of civilian casualties and the
"generation" of refugees.

Consider, in comparison, the American invest-
ment in care for the refugees and casualties. In the
summer of 1965, a subcommittee of the Senate
Judiciary Committee, entitled "Subcommittee on
Refugees" and chaired by Senator Edward M. Ken-

---

* In August, 1969, the Air Force Chief of Staff, Gen. John
P. McConnell, told the Senate Armed Services Committee: "Every
thing is operating up there [in North Vietnam] very nearly as if it
had not even been touched. I could say the repair is 75 per cent
completed."

nedy, held hearings on the refugee situation in South Vietnam, and these were followed by further investigations of both refugees and casualties in 1966 and 1967, a trip to Vietnam by Senator Kennedy in January, 1968, and a public report by the subcommittee in May, 1968.[19]

According to the Refugee Subcommittee's report, American financial support for the care and resettlement of refugees amounted to approximately $100-million for the three years 1966 to 1968 inclusive. Medical assistance for the civilian casualties totaled $76-million for the three years 1965 to 1967. Making generous allowance for missing figures, perhaps a quarter of a billion dollars was devoted to civilian relief during the four years 1965 to 1968, while military operations were at their peak. That is less than four per cent of the cost of air operations alone during the same period.

This parsimony in the "civil half" was observed when our own military actions were causing conditions in the refugee camps and hospitals that can only be described as frightful. Why? The Subcommittee found no rational answer:

> In many respects, the subcommittee has found this Government's handling of the civilian casualty and health problems one of the most puzzling aspects of our Vietnam involvement. The needs were obvious from the very early stages of our military buildup in Vietnam. Equally obvious was the fact that the South Vietnamese were themselves incapable of meeting the vast demands placed upon outdated and inadequate medical facilities.

*Yet for some reason this Government has been unable or unwilling to come to grips with the civilian medical situation in South Vietnam. We have talked of winning the hearts and minds of the people of South Vietnam; yet we have, we must assume by choice, chosen to meet only partially the urgent needs of the wounded, injured, and sick of this country we have sworn to help and these people we seek to protect. . . .*

It is, to be sure, much more the conventional military mission to fire guns and drop bombs than to build housing and hospitals. The fundamental mistake was not the Army's, but rather the selection of the Army to do a job for which it was ill-equipped. Once it was in charge, the worst aspects of the military system surfaced, then dominated the conduct of operations. Combat command is the surest road to promotion, and the Army and Air Force were only too glad to find a new theater for military experimentation. As Colonel Donovan describes the professional consequences:

*The highly trained career officers of the Army and the other services have found the Vietnam war a frustrating but fascinating professional challenge. The very size and scope of the American military force has also generated unceasing pressures to satisfy such military demands as trying out new weapons and using the war as a military testing ground and laboratory. Helicopter assault theories, air mobile operations concepts, new helicopter types, new*

*weapons and organizations, and counterinsur-
gency tactics were all ready for trial by the
Army in Vietnam. It was not a life-or-death war
in defense of the United States, but rather a
remote and limited conflict where training and
equipment could be tested and combat experience renewed or attained by the profession-
als. . . .*[20]

Perhaps stronger and wiser military leadership
would have averted the worst of the consequences,
or perhaps even advised against the entire venture,
in line with the views of generals such as Ridgeway
and Gavin. But the armed services no longer pos-
sess leaders of stature and influence comparable to
the heros of the Second World War. In the Army,
Marshall and MacArthur and their juniors such as
Eisenhower and Bradley, in the Navy, King and
Nimitz, in the air, Arnold, Spaatz and Doolittle
wielded moral as well as doctrinal influence, derived from their seniority, achievements and manifest ability. Today there are no comparable figures,
and in part this is due to the cheapening of rank.
After the victory over France in 1940, Adolf Hitler
cleverly robbed individual generals of laurels by
making them all field marshals and, to quote W. S.
Gilbert once again: "When everyone is somebody,
why no one's anybody." The spread of the "military-
industrial complex" has worked the same mischief
in our top military echelon today; there are so
many active and retired four-star "full" generals
that rank has lost its distinction, and so many retired senior officers employed by defense industries

(over 2,000 in 1969), that the rather Spartan simplicity of the old Army days has given way to a much more crass temper.

There are, to be sure, those who are able to regard the political consequences of American military operations in Vietnam as desirable. "In an absent-minded way," writes Professor Samuel P. Huntington, "the United States in Vietnam may well have stumbled upon the answer to 'wars of national liberation.' The effective response lies neither in the quest for conventional military victory nor in the esoteric doctrines of counterinsurgency warfare. It is instead forced-draft urbanization and modernization which rapidly brings the country in question out of the phase in which a rural revolutionary movement can hope to generate sufficient strength to come to power."[21]

But, as Professor Huntington elsewhere recognizes, the population shift to the cities is largely a flight from the horrors of war in the country. To describe the exodus stimulated by "zippo" raids and air strikes, and the consequent wretched huddle in refugee camps and hospitals, as "forced-draft urbanization and modernization" is a euphemism to end all euphemisms, fit to be bracketed with an American general's reported and less elegant judgment: "If you get them by the balls, the hearts and minds will follow."

What, then, are the obligations of the young man called by draft to serve in a war that he deeply believes to be, in the old religious terminology, "unjust"—whether because we had no right to inter-

vene in the first place, or because, in Colonel Donovan's words, our "techniques of fire and military
power were immoral and were in fact destroying
the people we were striving to assist"? Nuremberg,
historically speaking, gives no answer. But what
about Nuremberg the symbol of overriding international standards binding on individuals?

The Spanish theologians had a categorically affirmative answer to the question. "If a subject is
convinced of the injustice of a war, he ought not
to serve in it, even on the command of his prince,"
wrote Vitoria. "This is clear, for no one can authorize the killing of an innocent person. But in the case
before us the enemy are innocent. Therefore they
may not be killed . . . Hence flows the corollary
that subjects whose conscience is against the justice
of a war may not engage in it whether they be
right or wrong. This is clear for 'whatever is not of
faith is sin.' " Suarez was of the same opinion.[22]

To refuse to serve "even on the command of his
prince" is a high and principled standard—too high
for most men. Perhaps here the law will give some
sanctuary. It is true that the Selective Service statute gives conscientious objector status only to those
who are opposed to "war in any form," but today
there is distinguished authority for the view that,
at least in Vietnam ("a campaign fought with limited forces for limited objects with no likelihood
of a battlefront within this country and without a
declaration of war"), Congress cannot constitutionally require a man to do combat duty against the
dictates of his conscience.[23]

But we should not have to await an answer from

the courts. Given the course the war has taken, and
the depth and breadth of opposition to its conduct,
it is both unwise and inhumane to compel people
to serve in it against their will. For the United
States, this is a new kind of war for our times—the
precedents in Mexico and the Philippines are long
forgotten—and one for which compulsory service
should not be required.

In this respect, I believe, the views of the draft-
age generation are sound, and it is only to be re-
gretted that they have been so often pressed in a
counterproductive manner. I suppose that few
things have contributed more to the much-dis-
cussed "generation gap" than the circumstance that
most people over 45 were more or less deeply involved in the Second World War, the purposes and
waging of which they heartily approved, while no
one under 25 has any meaningful recollection of
any but the Vietnam war, which is widely regarded
as despicable and a national calamity. One need not
have been a hero to look back on military service in
World War II with satisfaction if not pride, and
with pleasure in feeling that one had made a contribution, however small, to a great and necessary
military victory. Given these memories, American
flag-burnings, Vietcong flag displays and shouts of
"Ho! Ho! Ho Chi Minh!" are bound to offend deeply
even those to whom the Vietnam war is an abomi-
nation. When one considers also the hundreds of
thousands of families whose sons have served in
Vietnam and perhaps been killed or wounded, and
who have a large psychological stake in the worth-
whileness of the sacrifice, bitter resentment and hos-

tility toward the uninhibited youth demonstrators are inevitable, as is the violence that is their product.

But it is not the demonstrations that cast the shadows of doubt and cynicism across those White House posthumous awards of Medals of Honor, and the countless memorials and mournings in humbler quarters; rather it is our own record as a nation, especially since 1964. It has been well said that a people get the kind of government they deserve. The Vietnam war was not the brain-child of construction workers, or Texas oilmen, or aircraft manufacturers, or super-patriots, or paranoid heresy-hunters. The war, in the massive, lethal dimensions it acquired after 1964, was the work of highly educated academics and administrators, most of whom would fit rather easily the present Vice-President's notion of an "effete snob." It was not President Kennedy himself, but the men he brought to Washington as advisers and who stayed on with President Johnson—the Rusks, McNamaras, Bundys, and Rostows—who must bear major responsibility for the war and the course it took.

"The contest in Vietnam is a contest for the allegiance of the South Vietnamese. No foreign force can win that battle. That is why the root of the struggle has always been in the South. That is why the bombing has always been marginal in its final meaning; that is why the necessities of American politics now coincide with the necessities of the South Vietnamese future." That is how McGeorge Bundy, one-time close adviser to President Johnson, saw the matter in October, 1968,[24] by which time he had concluded that "there is no prospect of military victory against North Vietnam by any level of U.S. military force which is acceptable," and that therefore the "burden of Vietnam" must be "lifted from our society."

Bundy was candid enough to acknowledge that "this has not always been my view," but nonetheless his recantation is oddly put. To *whom* does he wish the South Vietnamese to give "allegiance"? And are we to understand from the phrase "now coincide" that there was a time when the "necessities of American politics" did *not* coincide with the "necessities of the South Vietnamese future"? By what human calculation is bombing, and the consequent loss of life and limb, to be justified if it is "marginal in its final meaning"?

As one who until 1965 supported American intervention in Vietnam as an aggression-checking undertaking in the spirit of the United Nations Charter, I am painfully aware of the instability of individual judgment. Nevertheless, when the nature, scale and effect of intervention changed so drastically in 1965, it is more than "puzzling" (as the Senate Refugee Subcommittee put it) that virtually no one in high authority had the capacity and inclination to perceive and articulate the inevitable consequences. How could it ever have been thought that air strikes, free-fire zones and a mass uprooting and removal of the rural population were the way to win "the allegiance of the South Vietnamese"? By what mad cerebrations could a ratio of 28 to 1 between our investments in bombing, and in relief for those we had wounded and made homeless, have even been contemplated, let alone adopted as the operational pattern?

One may well echo the acrid French epigram, and say that all this "is worse than a crime, it is a blunder"—the most costly and tragic national blunder in American history. And so it has come to this: that the anti-aggression spirit of Nuremberg and the United Nations Charter is invoked to justify our venture in Vietnam, where we have smashed the country to bits, and will not even take the trouble to clean up the blood and rubble. None there will ever thank us; few elsewhere that do not now see our America as a sort of Steinbeckian "Lennie,"[25] gigantic and powerful, but prone to shatter what we try to save. Somehow we failed ourselves to learn the lessons we undertook to teach at Nuremberg, and that failure is today's American tragedy.

# Footnotes

## INTRODUCTION

1. A comprehensive review of this matter is contained in W. J. Bosch, *Judgment on Nuremberg: American Attitudes toward the Major German War-Crime Trials* (U. of N. Car. Press 1970).
2. *Pepper and Salt*, Supplementary Newsletter No. 3 (210 5th Ave., New York 10010), distributed June, 1970.

## CHAPTER 1

1. The history of American military practice with respect to the laws of war is covered in Colby, *War Crimes*, 23 Michigan Law Review 482, 606 (1925).
2. Department of the Army Field Manual FM 27–10, *The Law of Land Warfare* (1956). The 1940 edition was in effect during the Second World War.
3. G. Lowes Dickinson, *War: Its Nature, Cause, and Curse*, (1923), p. 16.
4. *Rules of Land Warfare*, War Dept. Doc. No. 467, Office of the Chief of Staff, approved April 25, 1914 (U.S. Gov't Printing Office 1917), par. 9.
5. *Op. cit. supra* note 2, at par. 3.

## CHAPTER 2

1. *Axtell's case*, 84 Eng. Rep. 1060 (1660).
2. Marshall's statement was made in *Little* v. *Bareme*, 2 Cranch 170, 179 (1804). For parallel decisions, see those of Justice Bushrod Washington in *United States* v. *Bright*, Fed. Cas. No. 14647 (C.C.D.Pa. 1809) and *United States* v. *Jones*, Fed. Cas. No. 15494 (C.C.D.Pa. 1813).
3. *United States* v. *Bevans*, Fed. Cas. No. 14589 (C.C.C. Mass. 1816). The case was tried in the Federal court on the jurisdictional basis that the crime occurred on the high seas. The Supreme Court reversed the conviction on the ground that Massachusetts Bay was not part

of the high seas, and therefore the Federal courts had no jurisdiction. *United States* v. *Bevans*, 3 Wheat. 336 (1818).

4. *Mitchell* v. *Harmony*, 13 How. 115, 137 (1851).

5. Story's observation is in *Martin* v. *Mott*, 12 Wheat. 19, 30 (1827), and Curtis' in *Despan* v. *Olney*, Fed. Cas. No. 3822 (C.C.D.R.I. 1852).

6. The proceedings of the military commission in the Wirz case were published in House Executive Documents, vol. 8, No. 23, Serial No. 1381, 40th Cong. 2d Sess. (1868). There is a vivid contemporaneous account of Andersonville and Libby prisons in A. C. Roach, *The Prisoner of War and How Treated* (Indianapolis, 1865). The play based on the trial, by Saul Levitt, is published by Dramatists Play Service, Inc. Those interested in the subject may also want to read McKinley Kantor's novel *Andersonville*, published in 1955.

7. The British provision is in *Manual of Military Law* (1914) p. 302, par. 366; the American is in *Rules of Land Warfare* (1917) p. 130, par. 366.

8. *Deutsche Allgemeine Zeitung*, 28 May 1944.

9. The 1944 revisions of the superior orders provisions of the British and American manuals are set forth in *History of the United Nations War Crimes Commission* (HMSO 1948), p. 282. The 1940 edition of the American Army's *Rules of Land Warfare* repeated (par. 347) the provision of the 1914 manual.

10. FM 27–10, *The Law of Warfare*, p. 182, par. 509, entitled "Defense of Superior Orders."

11. FM 27–10, *supra*, p. 178, par. 501. McClellan's order is quoted in Colby, *War Crimes*, 23 Michigan Law Review 482, at 502 (1925).

12. FM 27–10 *Rules of Land Warfare* (1940) pp. 89–90, par. 358.

CHAPTER 3

1. The quotations are from Eppstein, *The Catholic Tradition of the Law of Nations* (London 1935) p. 65. Other useful works on the relation between war and Christian

doctrine include Nussbaum, *Just War—A Legal Concept?* 42 Michigan Law Review 453 (1943); Von Elbe, *The Evolution of the Concept of the Just War in International Law,* 33 American Journal of International Law 665 (1939); Regout, *La Doctrine de Guerre Juste* (1934).

2. Grotius, *De Jure Belli ac Pacis* (1625).

3. The course of events with respect to war crimes charges of all descriptions following the First World War is set forth comprehensively and clearly in *History of the United Nations War Crimes Commission* (London, HMSO 1948).

4. There were other agreements and international resolutions to which the United States was a party that renounced war. Perhaps the most important was the resolution of the Sixth Pan-American Conference at Havana in 1928, which characterized "war of aggression" as "an international crime against the human species" and declared it "illicit" and "prohibited."

5. The discussion in the United Nations War Crimes Commission and its Legal Committee is set forth in the Commission's "History," *supra* note 3.

6. "Just War and Vatican Council II: A Critique" (Council on Religion and Industrial Affairs, 1966) p. 40.


CHAPTER 4

1. The essential facts concerning the establishment and activities of the Nuremberg and Tokyo tribunals may be found in Taylor, *Nuremberg Trials* (Carnegie Endowment for International Peace, 1949); Horwitz, *The Tokyo Trial* (Carnegie Endowment for International Peace, 1950); and the author's *Final Report to the Secretary of the Army on the Nuremberg War Crimes Trials under Control Council Law No. 10* (USGPO, 1949).

2. Georg Schwarzenberg, *The Breisach War Crime Trial of 1474,* in The Manchester Guardian, September 28, 1946; De Barante, *Histoire des Ducs de Bourgogne* (Paris 1837) vol. IX pp. 405–48, vol. X pp. 1–21.

3. Above, p. 16.

4. I Trial of the Major War Criminals before the International Military Tribunal (Nuremberg, 1947), p. 223.

5. The proceedings at the first Nuremberg trial are reported in the 42-volume series (the so-called "blue series") referred to in note 4, above. The proceedings at the ensuing trials are reported in the 15-volume series (known as the "green series") entitled *Trials of War Criminals before the Nuremberg Military Tribunals* (USGPO). A number of other important war crimes trials are reported in the 15-volume British series *Law Reports of Trials of War Criminals* (HMSO 1947–49).

6. The quotation is from the tribunal's judgment in *United States* v *von Leeb*, Case No. 12, vol. XI "Trials of War Criminals" at p. 489.

7. Above, pp. 36–38.

8. This is the so-called "Barbarossa jurisdiction order," signed by Field Marshal Wilhelm Keitel on May 15, 1941, and distributed throughout the German Army on the eastern front.

9. *In re Yamashita*, 327 U.S. 1 (1946). For a critical analysis of the trial see the book by one of Yamashita's defense counsel, A. Frank Reel, *The Case of General Yamashita* (1949). For the official rejoinder, see the Memorandum "The Case of General Yamashita" by Brig. Gen. Courtney Whitney, explaining the refusal to allow Reel's book to be translated and published in Japan, on the ground that "it is essential to guard against inflammatory material designed to arouse irresponsible Japanese elements into active opposition." There is an excellent book review by Charles S. Lyon, based on both the Reel and Whitney presentations, in 50 Columbia Law Review 393 (1950). For another unsuccessful effort to obtain Supreme Court review of procedural questions in war crimes trials, see the case of Yamashita's predecessor as commander-in-chief in the Philippines. *Homma* v. *United States*, 327 U.S. 759 (1946).

CHAPTER 5

1. The quotations are taken from the leading collection of materials on the legality of the Vietnam War, edited

by Richard Falk: *The Vietnam War and International Law,* 2 vol. (Princeton U. Press 1968).

2. The quotation from Eric Norden is from an article in *Liberation* (Feb. 1966) reprinted in Raskin and Fall, *The Vietnam Reader* (1967) pp. 432–33.

3. *International Conference on Military Trials* (USGPO 1947) pp. 294, 328, and 375.

4. U.N. Document A/CN. 425, dated 26 April, 1950.

5. New York Penal Law, Sections 35.15, 35.20, and 35.25; see also Model Penal Code of the American Law Institute, Sections 3.04, 3.05, and 3.06. Of course, force may also be used to enforce the law itself, or *in loco parentis.*

6. Falk, *supra* note 1, vol. 2, pp. 254–56.

7. Falk, *supra* note 1, vol. 2, p. 1069.

8. There is an excellent discussion of this and related questions in "Congress, the President, and the Power to Commit Forces to Combat," in 18 Harvard Law Review 1771 (1968). Marshall's comment is from his opinion in *Talbot* v. *Seeman,* 5 Cranch 1 (1801).

9. 54 Dept. of State Bulletin 474 (1966), reprinted in the Congressional Record, vol. 112, No. 43 (March 11, 1966). The view so stated is in line with President Johnson's own statement at a press conference on Aug. 18, 1967, and Under Secretary of State Nicholas Katzenbach's contemporaneous statement to the Senate Foreign Relations Committee. Falk, *supra* note 1, vol. 1, p. 711.

10. *Youngstown Sheet & Tube Co.* v. *Sawyer,* 343 U.S. 579 (1952).

11. *Luther* v. *Borden,* 7 How. 1, 42 (1849).

12. Wechsler, *Principles, Politics and Fundamental Law* (1961) pp. 11–13; Bickel, *The Least Dangerous Branch* (1962) pp. 69–70.

13. *Baker* v. *Carr,* 369 U.S. 186 (1962).

14. The two cases quoted are *Oetjen* v. *Central Leather Co.,* 246 U.S. 297 (1918) and *Johnson* v. *Eisentraeger,* 339 U.S. 763 (1950).

15. *Mora* v. *McNamara,* 389 U.S. 934 (1967).

16. *United States* v. *Sisson,* 294 Fed. Supp. 511 (D.Mass.

1968); to the same effect see *Velvel* v. *Johnson*, 287 Fed. Supp. 546 (D.Kans. 1968).

17. *United States* v. *Mitchell*, 386 U.S. 972 (1967).

18. *Head Money Cases*, 112 U.S. 580 (1884); *The Chinese Exclusion Case*, 130 U.S. 581 (1889); see *Reid* v. *Covert*, 354 U.S. 1, 18 (1957).

19. Falk, *supra* note 1, vol. 2, pp. 395–96.

20. Falk, *supra* note 1, vol. 2, p. 250.

21. Ferencz, "War Crimes Law and the Vietnam War," 17 American Univ. Law Review 403, 420 (1968).

CHAPTER 6

1. Barbara Tuchman, "End of a Dream—the United States, 1890–1902," from *The Proud Tower* (1966).

2. American operations in Quang Ngai province during the summer of 1967 are described in eye-witness terms in Jonathan Schell, *The Military Half–An Account of Destruction in Quang Ngai and Quang Tin* (1968), written shortly before the Son My incident occurred.

3. Two accounts of the Son My incidents which have been generally praised are Richard Hammer, *One Morning in the War—The Tragedy at Son My* (1970) and Seymour M. Hersh, *My Lai 4—A Report on the Massacre and its Aftermath* (1970). The narrative in the text is largely based on these two sources.

4. A useful compilation of the relevant treaties is "Treaties Governing Land Warfare," AFP 110–1–3 (Dep't. of the Air Force, 21 July 1958).

5. See, for example, the several essays and notes in Falk, *The Vietnam War and International Law*, vol. 2, pp. 361–593 (1969).

6. Lang, *Casualties of War* (1969), based on an article that appeared in *The New Yorker* on October 18, 1969.

7. Quoted in Falk, *supra* note 5 at pp. 539–40 and 547.

8. *United States* v. *List*, vol. XI, *Trials of War Criminals*, p. 1246; see also *United States* v. *Leeb*, vol. XI, *id.* pp. 529–32.

9. Falk, *supra* note 5, vol. 2, p. 240; see also the discussions by Lawrence Petrowski and Henry Meyrowitz, vol. 2, pp. 478–81 and 539–43.

10. *United States* v. *List, supra* note 8 at pp. 1308–09.

11. Hammer, *supra* note 8, p. 197.

12. Falk, *supra* note 5, vol. 2, pp. 450–51 and 564. The civil trial for damages is discussed and the opinion reproduced in English in Falk and Mendlovitz, *The Strategy of World Order* (1966) pp. 307 *et seq.* The case is entitled *Shimoda* v. *Japan,* 355 Hanrei Jiho 17 (Dec. 7, 1963); Japan was the defendant because, as part of the peace treaty with the United States, all claims of Japanese nationals against the United States were waived.

13. See Article 33 of the Geneva Convention for the Protection of Civilian Persons, and paragraph 272 of the Rules of Land Warfare, FM 27–10.

14. Falk, *supra* note 5, at p. 863.

15. Schell, *The Military Half,* pp. 119–81.

16. 1929 Geneva Convention, Article 2; 1949 Geneva Prisoners-of-War Convention, Article 13; Law of Land Warfare, FM 27–10, p. 177.

17. Falk, *supra* note 5, at p. 378, quoting 55 Dept. of State Bulletin 336, 338 (1966).

18. The contents of this paragraph are based on the reports in *The New York Times* between July 9 and July 19, 1970, under the by-lines of Robert M. Smith, Felix Belair Jr., and Gloria Emerson, as well as press service reports carried during the same period. See also the letter dated June 11, 1970, to *The New York Times* from Don Luce, former director of International Voluntary Services in Vietnam, reporting his observations of conditions in South Vietnamese prisons.

19. The paragraphs on the Duffy trial are based on the reports in *The New York Times* between March 28 and April 5, 1970, under the by-line of Philip Shabecoff.

20. *The New York Times,* June 22, 1970.


CHAPTER 7

1. Most of the material on the public reaction to Son My is based on Opton and Duckles, *My Lai: It Never Happened and Besides, They Deserved It* (Wright Institute, Berkeley, 1970), reproduced in abbreviated form in

*The New Republic,* Feb. 21, 1970. The authors utilized other surveys by the *Wall Street Journal* and *Time* magazine.

2. *Toth* v. *Quarles,* 350 U.S. 11 (1955). It may be that the discharged men involved at Son My could be tried before a special "military commission," or that the Federal courts might be given jurisdiction over such cases, but there are legal problems on either hand.

3. Taylor, *Two Studies in Constitutional Interpretation* (1969), Part II: *Fair Trial and Free Press;* Taylor, *Crime Reporting and Publicity of Criminal Proceedings,* 66 Columbia Law Rev. 34 (1966).

4. *Sheppard* v. *Maxwell,* 384 U.S. 333 (1966).

5. *The New York Times,* March 31, 1970, pp. 1 and 4, under the by-line of Philip Shabecoff.

6. The subcommittee's report is summarized in *The New York Times* of July 15 and 16, 1970. The report itself is entitled *Investigation of the My Lai Incident*—Report of the Armed Services Investigating Subcommittee, H. Rep. 91st Cong., 2d Sess., under H. Res. 105, July 15, 1970.

7. Report of The Department of the Army Review of the Preliminary Investigations into the My Lai incident (U), vol. 1, The Report of the Investigation, 14 March, 1970.

8. Reported in the *New York Post,* Feb. 7, 1968.

9. *San Francisco Chronicle,* Dec. 31, 1969, quoted in Opton and Duckles, *supra* note 1.

10. Hammer, *One Morning in the War,* pp. 70–71.

11. *The New York Times,* Jan. 1, 1970.

12. Falk, *The Vietnam War and International Law,* vol. 2, p. 494; Kolko, *War Crimes and the Nature of the Vietnam War* (1970), citing U.S. Senate, Committee on the Judiciary, *Hearings: Civilian Casualty, Social Welfare and Refugee Problems in South Vietnam.*

13. Falk, *supra* note 12, pp. 494 and 568; Donovan, *Militarism, USA* (1970), pp. 173–74.

14. Donovan, *supra,* p. 212.

15. William R. Corson, *The Changing Nature of War* (1970).

16. *United States* v. *von Leeb,* vol. XI Trials of War Criminals 374.

17. The initial Coburn-Cowan article entitled "The War Criminals Hedge their Bets" appeared in the *Village Voice* of Dec. 4, 1969. Mr. Hoopes's reply, "The Nuremberg Suggestion," was in the January, 1970, issue of *The Washington Monthly*, and the Coburn-Cowan reply was printed in the "letters" column the following month. Mr. Hoopes's book is *The Limits of Intervention—An Inside Account of how the Johnson Policy of Escalation in Vietnam was Reversed* (1969).

18. Hoopes, *The Limits of Intervention*, p. 51.

CHAPTER 8

1. Schlesinger, *The Bitter Heritage—Vietnam and American Democracy 1941–1966* (1967) p. 1.

2. The interview is described *in extenso* in *The New Yorker* of July 4, 1970.

3. See the pertinent passage in the Nuremberg "Justice Case," *United States* v. *Alstoetter*, vol. III Trials of War Criminals, pp. 979–82.

4. Hoopes, *The Limits of Intervention*, p. 29.

5. Hoopes, *supra*, p. 15.

6. Quoted in Donovan, *Militarism, USA*, p. 154.

7. Quoted in Schlesinger, *The Bitter Heritage*, p. 48.

8. Hoopes, *supra*, pp. 62–67 and 147.

9. Quoted from General Shoup's *Foreword* to Donovan, *Militarism, USA*, p. xiii.

10. *Supra*, p. 140.

11. Nuremberg Document NOKW-469, reproduced in part in volume XI Trials of War Criminals, pp. 831 and 1034–36.

12. Nuremberg Document NOKW-893, *id.* at p. 848.

13. Nuremberg Document NOKW-1487, *id.* at 847–48.

14. *The New York Times*, Jan. 22, 1970.

15. See, e.g., the *New York Post*, May 4, 1970.

16. *The New York Times*, Aug. 2, 1970.

17. Schell, *The Military Half*, pp. 197–198.

18. Donovan, *Militarism, USA*, pp. 178–80.

19. *Civilian Casualty and Refugee Problems in South Vietnam*, 90th Cong. 2d Sess., May 9, 1968.

20. Donovan, *supra* at p. 157.

21. Falk, *The Vietnam War and International Law,* vol. 2, p. 866.

22. The passage from Vitoria is taken from Eppstein, *The Catholic Tradition of the Law of Nations,* p. 103. *Suarez On War,* section VI.

23. The reference is to District Judge Charles Wyzanski's decision in *United States* v. *Sisson,* 297 F. Supp. 902 (D.Mass. 1969).

24. The quotation is from his address at DePauw University, Oct. 12, 1968, reprinted in Falk, *supra* note 21, at p. 974.

25. John Steinbeck, *Of Mice and Men, passim.*

# Index

223